A Higher Education

CASTING A GREATER VISION FOR
COLLEGE & BEYOND

Kimberly Wentzel

A Higher Education

Casting a Greater Vision for College & Beyond

© 2015 by Kimberly Wentzel. All rights reserved.

Trusted Books is an imprint of Deep River Books. The views expressed or implied in this work are those of the author. To learn more about Deep River Books, go online to www.DeepRiverBooks.com.

No part of this publication may be reproduced, stored in a retrieval system, or transmitted in any way by any means—electronic, mechanical, photocopy, recording, or otherwise—without the prior permission of the copyright holder, except as provided by USA copyright law.

Unless otherwise noted, all Scripture quotations are taken from the Holy Bible, New Living Translation, copyright ©1996, 2004, 2007, 2013 by Tyndale House Foundation. Used by permission of Tyndale House Publishers, Inc., Carol Stream, Illinois 60188. All rights reserved.

Scripture taken from The Holy Bible, New International Version®, NIV® Copyright © 1973, 1978, 1984, 2011 by Biblica, Inc.® Used by permission. All rights reserved worldwide.

Scripture taken from The Message. Copyright © 1993, 1994, 1995, 1996, 2000, 2001, 2002. Used by permission of NavPress Publishing Group." Bible.

Scripture taken from the New King James Version®. Copyright © 1982 by Thomas Nelson, Inc. Used by permission. All rights reserved

ISBN 13: 978-1-63269-407-2
Library of Congress Catalog Card Number: 2014960054

For Nate. Your solid faith is an
answered prayer. Keep casting a
greater vision for your life.
God is moving in big ways!

For James. Your love and
encouragement are invaluable.

For Kaden. May you grow to be
a strong man of God and embrace
His purpose for your life.

Contents

Acknowledgments ix

Introduction xi

1. Now Is the Time. 1
2. A Greater Vision 5
3. The Truth, the Whole Truth, and Nothing but the Truth 15
4. Living in Harmony 29
5. Set Yourself up for Spiritual Success 41
6. From the Inside Out 57
7. When It Rains… 79
8. Taming Temptation 87
9. Living with a Mission 93

Recommended Reading List. 99

Notes 101

Acknowledgments

Writing *A Higher Education* has been a long labor of love, and there are many, many people who've been involved in this journey that I need to thank. I appreciate every prayer, word of encouragement, and insightful thought that sparked an idea for this book. I have too many supporters to thank by name. However, there are a few key people who made invaluable contributions to this publication that I need to acknowledge.

First, a big thank-you to the whole creative team at Deep River Books for making this longtime dream a reality. You stepped in to save the day when I had lost all hope. Your commitment to do business with a Christ-like mind and heart is evident and appreciated.

Second, all my love and gratitude goes to my family for your unwavering encouragement and patience. I thank my parents for modeling what it means to make a living doing what you love and for always believing in me. I thank my wonderful husband for continually inspiring me and gently holding me accountable to finish this project. I thank my brother, Nate, for modeling many of the ideas found in this book. I'm sorry I couldn't finish it before you went to college, but you provided the perfect target audience, nonetheless. A simple "thank-you" feels insufficient as I express my gratitude to my mother-in-law, Nancy, for the many hours she spent editing this manuscript and preparing it for submission! You gave me the confidence to take the plunge into the publishing world.

Third, there have been a handful of teachers, ministers, and mentors who have been closely monitoring my progress and cheering me on from day one. Thanks to Mark Epperson and Dave Thorpe for welcoming me into your college ministry and challenging me to make my faith my own. It was during that year in Seekers that I finally caught a glimpse of what true Christian fellowship and discipleship look like and developed a love for studying God's Word! Thanks to Patrick and Nettie Langan for planting the seed that grew into a vision for this book. Your heart for college ministry and everything I learned through your mentorship provided much of the inspiration and substance for *A Higher Education*. Also, I want to give a big thanks to Ryan Cameron for always being in my corner and pushing me to cast a greater vision for the future.

Finally, and most importantly, I must thank the Lord for providing this humbling opportunity and continuing to guide and support me as I run the race. This project has never been about my desire to publish a book. My goal has always been to introduce students to the transformative love of Jesus Christ, and I pray that the Holy Spirit ignites a fire in their hearts that drives them to cast a greater vision for their futures. *Soli Deo Gloria.*

Introduction

Greetings! Chances are you're a new college student, a high schooler looking forward to post-grad life, or a parent of someone in this season. Either way, you're looking for help to navigate college life.

There are countless college self-help books out there. Many were written from a Christian platform. What makes this one unique? Most books I've read about thriving in college are written by professors and teach Christian kids to become successful students. They assume you have a solid foundation and work on your outer life, addressing important aspects of college life like time management and study skills.

But I come from a youth ministry background and know that the college years are a make-or-break time in your Christian walk. Students are stepping out from under the umbrella of their parents' faith and are beginning to ask tough questions. They have a million voices telling them what to believe. They need to learn to discern truth among the lies and decide for themselves who is the Lord of their life.

This book takes the term "Higher Education" quite literally. When thinking about your education, look beyond the textbooks, study schedules, parties, and career prep and see the bigger picture. Don't simply focus on what you want to do but ask yourself who you want to be. Don't merely survive college. Aim for God's best!

Learn what the Bible has to teach us about living well and apply it to every aspect of your college experience—the academic arena, your relationships, and how you handle the daily grind and weather life's storms. *A Higher Education* takes you on a journey that will challenge you to cast a greater vision for college and beyond!

I know your time is valuable, so this book is intentionally short and to the point. Each paragraph is full of hard-hitting principles designed to make you think. It's the kind of book you'll want to read with a highlighter, to wrestle with, and hopefully to discuss with your friends. If you're interested in digging deeper or reading stories about how students like yourself are challenging the status quo and daring to live for Christ on college campuses, check out my blog at:

AHigherEducationBook.com

Like *A Higher Education Book* on Facebook.

Follow me on Twitter @AHigherEdBook

I look forward to hearing about what the Lord is teaching you!

Blessings and Fruitful Reading,

—**Kimberly Wentzel**

1
Now Is the Time

Congratulations on finishing high school! I remember how I felt the day I received my diploma. I was on top of the world preparing to pursue my dreams and prove that I could succeed on my own. I'd always heard that the college years were the best of your life, and I couldn't wait for the fun to begin!

But then the story of my life took an unforeseen turn. All my lofty plans were put on hold as I underwent a major back operation two weeks after graduation. At the tender age of seventeen, I was faced with my own mortality. For the first time in my life, I had to ask the questions: What if I don't live to see tomorrow? What if this is it? What do I have to show for my time on this planet? Do I know for sure where I'll go after I die? I had to dig deep to overcome many fears and put my trust in God. I had no control over the situation, but He had the power and desire to do what was best for me. He was my only hope for a long and healthy future (see Jer. 29:11, Rom 8:28). The whole experience was painful. It was humbling. But it forced me to wrestle with these tough questions about life and faith, and it led me to a real, life-giving relationship with God.

Discovering how much I needed Him and seeing the world through His eyes before beginning my college career was a blessing. This revelation saved me from making several costly mistakes down the road. When I was smart enough to listen to my ever-present, compassionate, and trustworthy Friend, He never led me astray. He was my comfort in times of trouble and my companion in times of joy. My faith gave me hope and purpose—things often lacking in the collegiate community. I don't know how I would have made it through without Him.

My story has taken many unexpected twists and turns over the years, but God has faithfully carried me through every trial. I've been incredibly blessed, but I have many friends whose dreams for an illustrious future have been suddenly and permanently interrupted.

I'll never forget the day I received the devastating news about my best friend from high school. Josh and I were both film buffs with big Hollywood dreams. He met the love of his life while in college and proposed to her before they graduated. I still remember flipping through their engagement photos. I'd never seen him so happy!

Then out of the blue, I received a message from a mutual high school friend informing me that Josh had unexpectedly passed away. His death shocked many people in my graduating class because of our teenage sense of invulnerability. He was a special person that everyone liked and remembered with a smile. In an age of social media, I watched as friends and family from all over the country filled his memorial page with love, fond memories, and regrets over a bright future that would never be.

I still feel his loss deeply. But Josh isn't the only one whose life was cut short. In the eight years since I graduated from high school, six friends and classmates have died or suffered life-altering injuries. If there's one thing this season has taught me, it's that tomorrow is never a guarantee.

> So you, too, must keep watch! For you don't know what day your Lord is coming. Understand this: If a homeowner knew exactly when a burglar was coming, he would keep watch and not permit his house to be broken into. You also must be ready all the time, for the Son of Man will come when least expected.
>
> (Matt. 24:42-44)

Too often, people wait to focus on what matters most until after graduation. Then they need a job, so they procrastinate until their career takes off. Then life gets busy, so they drag their feet until they get married. Then they put it off until they have kids. We spend our entire lives looking forward to the day when we'll have the time or motivation to pursue God's best for our lives. Until then, we're in a holding pattern that keeps us occupied but unsatisfied.

The enemy wages an effective campaign against young believers by convincing them there will be time to live for God later. "Now is the time to study and party. Enjoy life while you have the freedom to do so and let your future self worry about eternity," he whispers.

Don't believe the enemy's lies! The time to start living wholeheartedly is now. Don't wait to pursue your passions and discover your calling. You may never get another chance. God has a plan and a purpose for you right now. He invites you to play a role in the rescue mission He's staging here on earth. Yes, your life matters! God wants, so badly, to draw you near and to transform you into the best possible version of yourself. So begin that process today! Consider it a Higher Education with eternal significance.

I felt so strongly about this that I started looking for opportunities to challenge others to ask those same tough questions and to strengthen their faith while in college. This passion to help others grow led me to youth ministry after graduation. Since my husband was in the Air Force, God called me to minister to military teens. This has presented me with a unique challenge, because these teens live in one place for only a couple of years. I have a very short amount of time to influence their lives and to help them understand who God is so they can decide for themselves if they will believe what the Bible says.

Their experience is somewhat similar to that of college students. Those getting a higher education have a limited number of years in school before stepping out into the world and needing to stand on their own two feet. The coming years will test them in every way a person can be tried. The goal is to mold them into intelligent, working adults. College is an all-consuming experience that affects more than just classwork. How do you embrace the great things college has to offer without losing track of what's most important—namely your faith in God? How do you grow as a person in addition to earning a degree?

A Higher Education

I pray you will be inspired to rise above the current collegiate norm of coasting through life. Grow and bear fruit as you work toward your degree. Go beyond college survival and thrive—academically, socially, and spiritually.

2
A Greater Vision

What do you want to be when you grow up? I bet you've had many different answers to that question over the years. I remember wanting to be a writer when I was five years old. At ten, I practiced cartwheels in my living room so I could become an Olympic gymnast like Kerri Strug. At thirteen, I took notes while watching HGTV because I was serious about pursuing a career in interior design. But during my freshman year of high school, I saw the movie *The Lord of the Rings: The Fellowship of the Ring* in theaters five times and fell in love with filmmaking. That dream stuck. I graduated from college with a degree in cinema and photography. But that doesn't mean the vision for my future didn't change during my university years. It did.

I changed a lot between my high school graduation and college graduation. In high school, our developmental focus was on external things like our appearance, grades, where we wanted to go in life, and what we wanted to do. Those things were easier to control, and they produced visible results. But our thoughts must turn inward as we face new challenges and begin to mature in college. We should no longer ask *what* we want to be but *who* we want to be and *why*.

The whole purpose of education is to better yourself by broadening your horizons, learning new things, and developing new skills. Unfortunately, many people limit their so-called higher education to the mere acquisition of information and the practical preparation for a career. While both are important, you can gain much more from your time in college than just knowledge. The sum total of your experience there—both inside and outside of the classroom—will shape you. The question is: What will you take away with you after graduation? Will you just be another university alum who is simply a bit older and smarter? Or are you striving for something more? As Richard Foster wrote, "The desperate need today is not for a greater number of intelligent people, or gifted people, but for deep people."[1]

In an economy where many people can't make full use of their degrees, I want you to walk away from college feeling that the time and effort you invested was completely worth it. Simply surviving won't give you that feeling. Challenge the status quo and cast a greater vision for your life!

The college selection process, these days, focuses mostly on you: what you've accomplished, where you want to go, what you want to do. But if you want your life to have true significance, it needs to mean something to others. Deep people look beyond the everyday and see the big picture. They desire more than their own happiness. They set their minds on higher things. College is a great place to begin making your life count for something because you still have the freedom to choose your path. As you're learning, growing, and being tested, your true character will start to develop. But you have to be very aware and intentional about the changes you undergo because it's all too easy to get distracted and lose your way.

Unfortunately, we live in a superficial society that encourages us to desire appealing but temporary things that only run skin-deep: wealth, fame, beauty, and power. This is especially true in the United States where we've had the American dream hammered into our heads since we were born. We spend our whole lives defending our liberties and pursuing trends that claim to lead to happiness. Somehow we've bought into the idea that our purpose in life is to be as successful and well liked as possible, so we use any means necessary to achieve the prosperity we believe we deserve. Too many people get wrapped up in the rat race and forget to focus on what matters most to them (faith, family, integrity) until it's too late. As Frederick Buechner once wrote, "The world is full of people who seem to have listened to the wrong voice and are now engaged in life-work in which they find no pleasure or purpose and who run the risk of

A Greater Vision

suddenly realizing someday that they have spent the only years that they are ever going to get in this world doing something which could not matter less to themselves or to anyone else."[2]

If you really want to go deeper and cast a greater vision for your life, you need to look beyond the material things you want and think about who you want to be. We have no guarantees in this lifetime. It could all be over in the blink of an eye. This uncomfortable truth should give us a sense of urgency when it comes to making choices. Be sure that you are not so focused on your pursuit of happiness that you lose track of who you're becoming. When the pleasure and prestige are stripped away, what are you left with? You can't take any earthly things with you when you die. "Everyone comes naked from their mother's womb, and as everyone comes, so they depart. They take nothing from their toil that they can carry in their hands" (Eccles. 5:15, NIV). So what will your enduring legacy be?

The key to overcoming our limitations and reaching our full potential is building a relationship with the One who has the power to make it happen. On our own, we're unable to go much deeper than the surface level. We are unable to achieve true and lasting significance. By nature, we focus exclusively on ourselves and our own needs, desires, and ambitions. But if we can't move past the stumbling block of our own self-interest, we'll miss out on innumerable opportunities to do something that matters. We were created with a purpose, and we can't fulfill it apart from the Creator, our God.

This craving to be great, which we all share, is one of the most tangible pieces of evidence we have that God is real. Our natural hunger for something more exists because there *is* something more. The One who breathed life into you loves you more than anything in the universe. He intentionally placed that inexplicable longing within you to lead you to Himself. As it says in the Bible, "He has planted eternity in the human heart" (Eccles. 3:11).

We were made to enjoy an everlasting relationship with God. Without it we feel empty and have a sense that something's missing. You might try to fill that hole in your chest with success, romance, drinking, or drugs, but nothing helps. Advertisers capitalize on this emptiness and try to convince you that if you just buy or do more, you'll be happy. But that vital spot in your heart is reserved for God and God alone. The more you fight it, the bigger and more painful the hole grows. Trust me, I know. Every time I try to do things for myself and leave God out of the equation, nothing seems to go the way it should. I end up more frustrated, broken, and lonely than I was before. I'm sure you've experienced something similar.

But once you accept the fact that God sent His Son to die so you could be free from your sin, a huge weight will lift from your shoulders. The good news of the gospel is that you're not alone. He will comfort, strengthen, and guide you as no human being can. You don't have to manufacture your own significance. God proved how valuable you are when He sacrificed His beloved Son to save you and to give you a future.

As you spend more time learning about our Savior and listening to His words, you'll begin to understand the grand vision He has for your life—a life full of promise and purpose. "'For I know the plans I have for you,' declares the LORD, 'plans to prosper you and not to harm you, plans to give you hope and a future'" (Jer. 29:11, NIV). He knows you better than you know yourself and will help you live life to the fullest. Even your wildest dreams can't compare to what He has in store for you. But in order to discover that plan, you have to invite Him into your life and put Him in control.

When I graduated from high school, I had life figured out. God called me to inspire others, and He gave me a passion for storytelling. I planned to study filmmaking in college and then move to Los Angeles and spark a spiritual revolution in Hollywood. I'd be the first female to win an Oscar for best director and give God the credit on live television. I thought I'd be bringing glory to God in a place where He was not welcome. But really my dreams stemmed from my pride and craving for praise and recognition.

The summer after my senior year, God got my attention by putting my college plans on hold with some pressing health concerns. While all my friends moved into newly decorated dorm rooms and started taking classes, I was stuck at home recovering from major back surgery. I couldn't understand why God was holding me back. I'd lost control of both my body and my future plans.

He stripped me of everything I turned to for strength, comfort, or guidance, which forced me to solely rely on Christ for everything. Learning to trust Him took a long time. But in the process, I stepped out from underneath the protective shelter of my parents' faith and cultivated my own. I encountered my Savior in a very real way and fell head-over-heels in love with Him.

Suddenly I was less concerned about asserting my own greatness and more interested in helping others understand how great our God was. Instead of making plans, I asked Him to direct me down the best path for my life. So far, His route has headed in the opposite direction of what I would've chosen. Instead of making movies, I married an Air Force pilot, and we're constantly moving all over the world. At each duty station, God provides a way for me to use my gifts to expand His ministry to women and teens. I haven't won an Oscar yet, but I have a loving husband, an adventurous, international lifestyle, an adorable baby, and a job that's far more rewarding than anything I could have envisioned when I was eighteen. I'm so thankful that God gave me the courage to take my hands off the wheel of my life and to let Him show me the way.

"Giving God the wheel" translates to "Lordship" in spiritual lingo and is one of the most important things to consider when preparing for college. Your purpose and direction in life stem from Him, and that should heavily influence where you choose to go to school and what you major in as well as what clubs or activities you join. The best path differs for every person. If you're struggling to find your way, ask God what He wants you to do. That may sound simplistic, but it works. We may not be able to sit down and have a conversation with Jesus like the disciples did. But He gave us the Holy Spirit so that all of His future followers would have access to the Father's direction. The Holy Spirit is intimately connected to God. So everything He conveys to us through the Bible, prayer, or other believers is trustworthy. The Bible says, "When the Spirit of truth comes, He will guide you in all truth. He will not speak on His own but will tell you what He has heard. He will tell you about the future. He will bring Me glory by telling you whatever He receives from me" (John 16:13-14).

Spiritual guidance is rarely straightforward. God speaks in multiple ways. But if you've sought what He says on the subject in the Bible, prayed about it, and talked with others who know the Lord and have your best interests at heart, you're well on your way to making a sound decision. Sometimes what seems logical or makes sense according to worldly wisdom is not right for you. It could be that you're all set to go, but something just doesn't feel right. If so, you may need to reevaluate. Fortunately, God is always available to talk to when you feel lost or overwhelmed. It says in the Bible that "If any of you lacks wisdom, you should ask God, who gives generously to all without finding fault, and it will be given to you" (James 1:5, NIV).

Don't stress too much about where to go to college and what career to pursue. Sometimes young believers are afraid to make a move in case they misunderstand what God wants and inadvertently derail His plan for their life. Don't worry! God outlines what He desires from us clearly in the Bible, and it might help you to know that what He desires most is not limited to super-specific details like what school to attend or declaring a major. Jesus explains in Luke 10:27 that the two greatest commandments are to: "Love the Lord your God with all your heart and with all your soul and with all your strength and with all your mind" and, "Love your neighbor as yourself'" (NIV). In terms of what He wants you to do with your life, Jesus says, "I have been given all authority in heaven and on earth. Therefore, go and make disciples of all the nations, baptizing them in the name of the Father and the Son and the Holy Spirit. Teach these new disciples to obey all the commands I have given you" (Matt. 28:18-20).

This last verse is called "The Great Commission," and it sums up our purpose. We have been put on this earth to love and serve others and to tell them about our God so they will be saved. We can accomplish this anywhere with or without a degree, and our mission will continue until the end of our days. Instead of worrying about the one place that will be a perfect fit, ask God to show you where He can best use you. If it turns out that the school you chose isn't working out, then maybe He's calling you elsewhere. It's important to understand that whatever your circumstances or wherever God

A Greater Vision

leads you, He has placed you there for a reason and wants to do great things through you if you will let Him!

At this point, you may feel you have gotten more than you bargained for with this book. You wanted to learn how to have an awesome time in college, and I'm talking about giving up your control to an all-powerful God and helping Him save lives! You're already struggling to balance classes, sports, work, and relationships without having to worry about other people's salvation! But that's exactly why the subject of this book is so important.

When we feel overwhelmed, it's easy to switch into survival mode and only do what it takes to get through the day. I notoriously bite off more than I can chew. Ambition, combined with an inability to say no, regularly wrecks my equilibrium and sleep schedule. As my to-do list grows, I prioritize my time to meet deadlines instead of focusing on what's most important. I may feel I have accomplished something at the end of a hectic day because I checked several items off the list. But in the long-run, my spiritual, physical, and emotional health suffers when I operate in survival mode. I stop getting my fill of God and burn out quickly. When I tough it out, relying solely on my own strength, the best I ever achieve is average.

God's plan for you is to thrive, not just survive! Jesus says in John 10:10, "I am the Gate. Anyone who goes through me will be cared for—will freely go in and out and find pasture. A thief is only there to steal and kill and destroy. I came so they can have real and eternal life, more and better life than they ever dreamed of" (MSG). You have greatness in you; you just need to know how to unleash it! How do I know? If you have a relationship with Jesus Christ, you have the Holy Spirit of God inside you to guide you and empower you to make an impact. True greatness doesn't lie in making a fortune or a name for yourself; it comes from living for the glory of God and leaving a deep imprint on the people around you.

Once you really get to know the living God and start to live for Him, you'll never want to go back. You may not have met this God before, but He wants you to know and trust Him! He's a God who desires to give you more than you could ever dream of asking for yourself (see 1 Cor. 2:9). He's a God with a monumental plan for your life. And He's a God who is willing and able to do miracles through everyday people like you.

Don't believe me? Try reading through some of the best-loved stories of the Bible. Moses was an orphan and a murderer, but God used him to save an entire nation. David was a shepherd boy who defeated a giant and became one of the most celebrated kings of all time. Mary was a simple girl engaged to a carpenter. But of all the women in history, God chose her to be the mother of the Savior of the world! Imagine what He could do in and through you!

In his best-selling book *The Prayer of Jabez for Teens*, Bruce Wilkinson goes into detail about the difference God can make in a young person's life when he or she is willing to give his or her life to Him. I've been inspired by this book many times and can never get over the following passage: "God really does have an extraordinary life waiting for you. He's been planning all the great things you will do for Him since before you were even born! (Eph. 2:10). All you have to do is want His best for your life . . . and ask for it with all your heart."[3]

God wants you to be ambitious and to dream big! We just need to make sure that our desire is to bring Him glory and to serve others rather than merely serving and glorifying ourselves. That's the mark of true depth and maturity: when we're able to move beyond a self-serving attitude and to place the needs of others before our own. Translate that general goal into a thousand different things. You can glorify God as an athlete, teacher, astronaut, or even as president of the United States. The possibilities are endless. He has the power, so throw all your fears and limitations out the window. Nothing is impossible with God!

I love what Chip Ingram says in his book *Good to Great in God's Eyes*: "Great accomplishments usually begin with the pursuit of a dream."[4] Sometimes God will help you achieve your specific goals. Sometimes He'll redirect you, along the way, until you discover something even better. But either way, God wants to do big things in you!

I experienced this personally while in college. I knew that God had called me to inspire people. He used my love of movies to draw me to the college's school and campus ministry. This ministry introduced me to the importance of reaching out to teens and young adults. Now I use my knowledge, creativity, and skills to inspire people through writing instead of through movies. I hope that one day God will give me an opportunity to work on a major motion picture, but I have no doubt that the path I'm on now is the right one. My dreams haven't turned out the way I had planned, but I wouldn't have accomplished anything great without first believing that God could use me in a big way.

So what do you want to do? Who do you want to be? You may have dismissed some of your biggest dreams a long time ago because they seemed foolish or impossible. But just as God planted eternity in your heart, He also sowed some element of that dream as a part of His perfect design. "To fulfill His purposes and build His kingdom, God will first and foremost direct His energy toward one thing: captivating your heart with great dreams."[5]

As you embark on your college career, I challenge you to go beyond thinking about applications and employment and to dream a little. Cast a greater vision for your future! The next few years of your life will define you as an individual and as an adult. Will you try to do things the world's way and see what happens? Or will you take the plunge and allow God to guide you down the road to everlasting glory? His way may not always be easy or comfortable. Sometimes the path to your greatest potential lies straight through your biggest fear.[6] But I assure you that the end result is one hundred percent worth it. What do you say? The choice is yours.

3
The Truth, the Whole Truth, and Nothing but the Truth

Most college students these days can't function without coffee or a similar stimulant to jump-start their day. Some like their coffee steaming hot. Some like it iced. But I don't know anyone who craves leftover, room temperature, lukewarm coffee. Gross!

I'm not much of a coffee drinker. One swig of even the weakest, most chocolate infused coffee concoction and I make a face like a kid drinking cough syrup. But I do love coffee shops. There's nothing better than sitting at a Starbucks and having a deep discussion with friends. Something about that atmosphere fosters intimate conversation and self-reflection. Every once in a while, someone asks a question that inspires me or challenges me to grow. For example, this question recently rocked my world: Would your life look any different if you were to suddenly stop believing in God?

Sadly, my answer was no, not really. I would still live in the same place with most of the same friends and go about the same daily routine without much change in habits or behavior. Most people would probably see me as a good person, but I want to be more than that. I want my faith to make a big difference, not only in my life but in the lives of everyone I encounter. I want it to be obvious that I'm different because the Holy Spirit is working in me. But to be honest, I'm lukewarm most of the time. In Revelation 3, Jesus addresses people like me. "I know all the things you do, that you are neither hot nor cold. I wish that you were one or the other! But since you are like lukewarm water, neither hot nor cold, I will spit you out of my mouth! I correct and discipline everyone I love. So be diligent and turn from your indifference" (Rev. 3:15-16, 19).

Why do Christians find it so easy to be lukewarm and indifferent in their relationship with the Almighty? Popular pastor and author Francis Chan attributes it to our inaccurate view of God. "We see Him as a benevolent Being who is satisfied when people manage to fit Him into their lives in some small way."[1] We get focused on the comfortable parts of God because that makes our role easier. Somehow we begin to picture Jesus as this gentle, loving man whose arms are always full of lambs and children and who is eager to pat us on the back when we make the effort to go to church or talk to Him for five minutes before we pass out at night (OK, maybe five minutes is a generous number).

We forget that God is the Alpha and the Omega, the Creator of the universe and everything in it. He holds all power and authority in heaven and on earth, and while He loves and redeems us, He also requires our complete, unwavering allegiance. "Understand, therefore, that the LORD your God is indeed God. He is the faithful God who keeps His covenant for a thousand generations and lavishes his unfailing love on those who love Him and obey His commands" (Deut. 7:9). He often asks us to do difficult things that push us outside our comfort zone, so we develop selective memory and pick and choose the parts of the Gospel that make us feel good.

For example, we focus on how much Jesus loves us and the forgiveness He offers. We feel secure knowing that no matter what we do, He'll always love us and forgive us of our sins. It's easy to feel good about your lifestyle when you follow a loving, permissive God. But we tend to gloss over that pesky passage in Matthew 7 that says, "Not everyone who calls out to me, 'Lord! Lord!' will enter the Kingdom of Heaven. *Only those who actually do the will of my Father in heaven will enter.* On judgment day many will say to me, 'Lord! Lord! We prophesied in your name and cast out demons in your name and performed many miracles in your name.' But I will reply, 'I never knew you. Get away from me, you who break God's laws'" (Matt. 7:21-23, emphasis added).

The Truth, the Whole Truth, and Nothing but the Truth

When I was in college, it was popular to point out that Jesus' first miracle was turning water into wine. He also used wine to illustrate that His blood was about to be poured out for our sins, during the Last Supper. So they reasoned Jesus must be OK with drinking, right? It does say in Ecclesiastes that, "A man can do nothing better than to eat and drink and find satisfaction in his work" (Eccles. 2:24, NIV). But Jesus and His apostles caution us repeatedly not to take it too far and get drunk. We should never allow any of our sinful desires to control us instead of the Holy Spirit. Once we give our life to Christ, our goal should always be to please God instead of indulging in sinful impulses. As it says in Romans, "Those who are dominated by the sinful nature think about sinful things, but those who are controlled by the Holy Spirit think about things that please the Spirit. So letting your sinful nature control your mind leads to death. But letting the Spirit control your mind leads to life and peace" (8:5-6). Deciding where to draw the line with things like alcohol is tricky. In Christ we have great freedom, but not everything is beneficial (see 1 Cor. 10:23). When we choose to hold firmly to some passages in scripture but overlook others in order to live the way we want to, we head into dangerous territory.

While our selective memory may be a little easier on our conscience, we're not doing anyone any favors by failing to embrace God and His Truth entirely. We're not honoring God completely with our lives. We hinder Him from working in us and filling us with His abundant love. Worst of all, by not completely committing ourselves to Him, we show the world a weak, hypocritical sliver of what following Christ means and push them away from the true God instead of drawing them in. Jesus isn't interested in people who are on the fence, testing the waters of faith with a toe while their other foot is solidly planted in the world. As He says in Matthew 6:24, "No one can serve two masters. For you will hate one and love the other; you will be devoted to one and despise the other." In that context He was referring to the conflict between the love of God and money. But money is only one of many earthly attachments that prevent us from being effective in our faith and ministry.

Think about the people whose faith you really admire. What is it about their walk with Jesus that caught your attention? My husband and I met a couple in college named Dave and Claire, who set the standard for living as God desires. They're the type of people you can't help but love. They both have a great sense of humor. Dave is an artist and a musician, and they both sing and dance. They have that kind of open, friendly, goofy personality that makes every outing fun. They're not just entertaining, they're joyful, and it's contagious! They'd be the first to tell you they're not perfect. But you can tell there is something about their faith that is different. Evangelism is not work to them. The gospel is the core of their identity, so their love for Jesus naturally colors everything they do and say. Anyone could spend an afternoon with them and walk away wanting whatever it is that makes them so awesome.

Authentic, compelling Christianity consists of more than just love and fuzzy feelings. It's more than following rules or trying to be good. It involves knowing the truth and devoting yourself to it one hundred percent. The gospel defines who you are and what you're meant to do on earth. Nothing matters more than your relationship with Christ. So ask yourself, would your life look any different today if you suddenly stopped believing in God? If not, read the Word and pray, asking God to change your heart so that all will know, without question, who is the Lord of your life.

There's no time to waste. For all you know, today will be the day He calls you home. Can you afford to ignore what God is calling you to do? As a college student, you are in the perfect position to start taking this seriously and revolutionize your walk with God.

What do you say? Are you craving more than the same old lukewarm spirituality that does nothing for you? Or do you dare to be different? Will you throw earthly wisdom aside and stake everything on the cross?

In the fourth century, a man named Athanasius stood against popular thinking to defend the truth that Jesus Christ was the incarnate Son of God. The Catholic Church declared him a saint, and he soon became a symbol of standing up for your beliefs. He was known as Athanasius Contra mundum, which means "Athanasius against the world."[2] *Contra Mundum* is the battle cry of men and women who turn their backs on this sinful world and commit themselves to following Christ wholeheartedly.

Turning our back on the world may sound harsh. Why do we have to do that in order to be a Christian? Eric Ludy makes a great point in his book *The Bravehearted Gospel*. "There is a simple truth in the kingdom of God: the more beautiful and stunning you are to the world, the more disagreeable you are in the eyes of Heaven . . . Heaven and earth represent two contrary systems and they are at odds with one another. It never ceases to amaze me why any of us as Christians ever spend even a moment's time considering what this world thinks about us."[3]

There's something wrong when our lives look just like those of our unbelieving friends and neighbors. My husband and I often struggle with trying to behave in a Christlike manner while hanging out with our non-believing friends. Many traditions, activities, and behaviors common in the military community, and particularly among fighter pilots, don't glorify God. One night in a Bible study, we were wrestling with where to draw the line. How could we connect with people and participate in social functions without getting sucked into sinful behavior? We needed a way to gauge how well we were living out our faith. Then our friend Mark said something that I will never forget, "If people would be shocked to find out that you're a Christian, you know that you're in trouble."

We struggle because we want to fit in and have friends and be liked. But God didn't call us to be liked, He called us to be salt and light (see Matt. 5:13-16). We think we can accomplish both—have a solid faith but never ruffle anyone's feathers. But as Ben Davenport pointed out in his intro to *The Bravehearted Gospel* (paraphrased here), I don't know how we came to that conclusion when Jesus, the most perfect and loving Being ever to walk this earth, was murdered by the people we're trying to impress.[4] Jesus was clear on this point, "If you belonged to the world, it would love you as its own. As it is, you *do not* belong to the world, but I have chosen you *out of* the world. That is why the world hates you. Remember what I told you:

'A servant is not greater than his master.' If they persecuted Me, they will persecute you also" (John 15:19-20, NIV, emphasis added).

Why didn't people like Jesus? He didn't play by the world's rules. He didn't look or act the way they thought a leader should. Jesus was not attractive by the world's standards (see Isa. 53:2). He was the son of a carpenter, born in a barn. He hung out with a vagrant band of nobodies and was beaten and executed as a criminal. But God had the whole thing planned from the beginning. He orchestrated everything, from Jesus' humble entrance into the world to his humiliating exit, to make a point. God doesn't need the strongest, most popular, or wealthy people on His side to get things done. He purposely chooses underdogs, so when they work miracles, it's clear who deserves the credit. "Brothers and sisters, think of what you were when you were called. Not many of you were wise by human standards; not many were influential; not many were of noble birth. But God chose the foolish things of the world to shame the wise; God chose the weak things of the world to shame the strong. . . . so that no one may boast before Him" (1 Cor. 1:26-27, 29, NIV).

If we're not aiming to be comfortable or popular or simply moral, what is the point of our faith? Why did Jesus come to earth in the first place? We've already established that He came to save us from our sins and to give us eternal life. But in John 18:37, when Jesus is being interrogated before His crucifixion, He shares His primary mission statement. "The reason I was born and came into the world is to testify to the truth. Everyone on the side of truth listens to me" (NIV). In that scene, Pilate follows this incredible statement with a skeptical question we all know well: "What is truth?"

This is one of the most important questions we need to answer as a culture, as individuals, and as believers. We've grown up in a time when the definition of truth, which was once concrete, is becoming harder to pinpoint. People either don't believe in truth or think we all have our own personal truth and shouldn't presume to tell anyone what is right and wrong. This may sound smart and agreeable, since it helps us avoid the discomfort of confrontation, labels, and rules. But we honestly can't live in a world like that.

The Truth, the Whole Truth, and Nothing but the Truth

Truth, according to dictionary.com, is "conformity with fact or reality." But if everyone has a different version of truth, how can we know that anything is real? For example, you may say the sky is blue. But what if I believe it's really green? And another person swears it's red? If there is no such thing as a verifiable fact, how can we study or understand the world around us? How can we know what is right or wrong without standards we can trust? Our society, government, schools, and relationships depend on the stability that the truth creates.

Dr. Del Tackett, front man for Focus on the Family's revolutionary series called The Truth Project,[5] gives us this definition: Truth is an affirmation of what God sees as reality. Without God, we can't answer all these major questions in life beyond the shadow of a doubt. He is the creator of everything in the universe. Without His Spirit of truth guiding us, we find it too easy to invent our own version of reality.

Satan uses subtle lies as his most effective tool for keeping humans blind to the truth. They are deceptive and often completely factual according to our best worldly knowledge. But because these claims of truth completely leave God out of the picture, they are lies all the same. "They traded the truth about God for a lie. So they worshiped and served the things God created instead of the Creator himself, who is worthy of eternal praise!" (Rom. 1:25). We need to use God and the Bible as a reference point to evaluate everything we see and learn and experience so we can know what is true and false. Recognizing the truth and owning it for ourselves will protect us from the devil's cunning and treacherous reasoning, which I guarantee you will frequently encounter in college.

The enemy has planted a very strong and subtle lie within this popular cultural belief: Always follow your heart. Instead of relying on biblical truth, we're taught to trust our gut and do whatever feels right. We can't be faulted for a decision that we're sure was the right one for us at the time. This philosophy sounds great on the surface. No other person knows your needs and desires better than you, so don't let anyone pressure you into doing something you know is wrong. When our hearts belong one hundred percent to Christ, this policy will never fail. But since none of us is perfect, we must be cautious. Our feelings and urges often can't be trusted. We have a sin nature and struggle to keep our evil desires in check. Even after entering into a relationship with Jesus, Paul, a spiritual rock star, still struggled.

> What I don't understand about myself is that I decide one way, but then I act another, doing things I absolutely despise. So if I can't be trusted to figure out what is best for myself and then do it, it becomes obvious that God's command is necessary . . . For if I know the law but still can't keep it, and if the power of sin within me keeps sabotaging my best intentions, I obviously need help! . . . I decide to do good, but I don't *really* do it; I decide not to do bad, but then I do it anyway. My decisions, such as they are, don't result in actions. Something has gone wrong deep within me and gets the better of me every time.
> (Rom. 7:15-20, MSG)

How do we know that a gut feeling is really what God wants us to do versus what our hormones and sinful desires are prompting us to do? Satan is an expert at manipulating our emotions in order to keep us focused on ourselves and fulfilling our own plans rather than following God's plan for our lives. This is only one example of a subtle, but deadly, lie masked in widely accepted truth.

We are lied to constantly: Man is basically good. Having more money and power and sex will make us happier. The most important thing is to look out for our own self-interest. But that's not what we see when we step out our front door. We live in a broken world, and no matter how much time passes or what kind of new technological advances we make or laws we pass, we keep running into the same problems. The news has been a broken record for generations. We're still lying, cheating, and stabbing each other in the back (both literally and figuratively). Yet the enemy wants us to believe that if we're in bondage, it can be fixed if we try harder. The truth is that we are all naturally wicked and need God desperately if we want to escape this cycle of pain and death and step into the light.

The Truth, the Whole Truth, and Nothing but the Truth

The earlier you figure this out, the better. Dr. Tackett wisely points out that every sin can be traced back to a belief in a lie.[6] For example, if a girl believes that her beauty and value are measured by male attention instead of God's love for her, it's likely she'll be tempted to compromise herself physically. If a guy buys into society's standard for success, he'll likely focus his attention on making money and building himself up instead of glorifying God. If we mistakenly believe that some sins are worse than others, we can justify telling little, white lies and gossiping about our friends. It's not like we murdered someone. If following our heart is more important than respecting authority, we don't need to feel bad about disobeying our parents. Satan is so good at convincing us to think and act in ways that are contrary to God's Word. It's so much easier to go with the flow and conform to societal norms than to stand up for what is right and true.

What can we do to defend ourselves from this ceaseless, enticing attack? The apostle Paul provides an answer in the book of Ephesians that sounds like the philosophy of a hero like William Wallace[7].

> Put on the full armor of God, so that you can take your stand against the devil's schemes . . . Stand firm then, with the belt of truth buckled around your waist, with the breastplate of righteousness in place, and with your feet fitted with the readiness that comes from the gospel of peace. In addition to all this, take up the shield of faith, with which you can extinguish all the flaming arrows of the evil one. Take the helmet of salvation and the sword of the Spirit, which is the word of God.
> (Eph. 6:11,14-17, NIV)

The next time the devil is tempting you, picture yourself in blue face paint and tell him that he may take your life (or popularity, etc.), but he'll never take your freedom!

We need to find the courage and motivation to change the way we think and live. Have the guts to let go of the world's lies. Instead of buying into secular thinking, root your beliefs in the

Holy Spirit so you'll grow and thrive. "Don't copy the behavior and customs of this world, but let God transform you into a new person by changing the way you think" (Rom. 12:2).

Change isn't easy. Letting go of long-held beliefs and living in a way that is totally opposite of what everyone else is doing can be painful. But that's exactly what God calls us to do. We must step out of our comfort zone, turn from our former ways, and embrace the *best* way.

Eugene Peterson says in his book *A Long Obedience in the Same Direction* that you need to come to the "realization that what God wants from you and what you want from God are not going to be achieved by doing the same old things."[8] That's what it means to repent: to completely turn your back on your old sinful ways and run to God. It's not easy, and until you've become completely disgusted with the ways of the world, it will be difficult to find the strength to follow in Christ's footsteps. But that decision is the key to discovering the absolute best this life has to offer.

This change is not a onetime decision. It often involves making the choice to do what's right, over and over again throughout the day until God's way becomes a habit. For example, I hate gossip. I know it's wrong and how hurtful it is when I hear others talking about me and my friends behind our backs. You'd think it'd be easy for me to avoid the sin I despise. After all, I'm a Christian! But if you put me in a room with my girlfriends, and one of them starts gossiping, it's really hard not to join in. Often, I give in and start laughing and telling stories without even realizing what I'm doing. I'm sure you can relate! It wasn't until a close friend called me out on my hypocrisy and I felt completely disgusted with my sin that I was able to take a personal stand against gossiping. I can't say that my track record has been perfect since then. (Far from it!) But I now make a conscious effort to censor my words and exclusively think and speak of my friends in a loving, godly way.

You may know in your head that it's important to repent. But that head knowledge won't make a difference unless you know yourself and are willing to invite God into your heart and mind and start cleaning house. Once you take the time to actually think through everything God's taught you and how it applies to your life, it will be much easier to make those necessary changes. Your belief will direct your steps. That's why it's so important to do some soul-searching while you're in college and to decide, once and for all, where you stand. Don't shy away from tough questions. They can lead you to a stronger faith that will stand the test of time.

Ask yourself if you really believe what the Bible claims to be true, is true. Do you believe, deep down, that God created the heavens and the earth? That Jesus died on the cross to set you free? That He is the way, the truth, and the life, and no one will come to the Father except through a relationship with Him? (see John 14:6) That because Jesus rose from the grave, you have the Holy Spirit within you, who gives you the power to do even greater works than He did on earth? (see John 14:12; Acts 1:8) That greater is He that is in you than He that is in the world (see 1 John 4:4)?

Imagine how different the world would be if we, as Christ-followers, really believed what we preached. Jesus said it himself, "I tell you the truth, if you had faith even as small as a mustard seed, you could say to this mountain, 'move from here to there,' and it would move. Nothing would be impossible" (Matt. 17:20). What do your actions reveal about the size of your faith and your commitment to the truth? What kind of risks do you take to follow in Christ's footsteps? How many people have you shared the good news with? How could you make a difference in your community if you stopped apologizing for being a Christian and put your confidence in the cross?

Human beings have been struggling with the enormity and implications of these big life questions for centuries. We seem to be on a constant quest for what scholars call the universal truths. If people could just stop running from the face of God and accept His truth, which is real, the quest would end, and we could start moving forward.

Unfortunately, Christianity today is anti-intellectual. We keep trying to reconcile the claims of modern science with the truth of the Bible. Who would have thought that dinosaurs and apes could cause such a crisis of faith? Somehow, what scientists observe and currently believe about the world has become unquestionable fact, and anyone who thinks differently is ignorant. Religious belief has been downgraded from a valid world view to a private matter of the heart. We've moved faith out of the public sector and safely stowed it behind closed doors where we can't offend anyone and they can't criticize us any longer.

The trend seems to say that if we want to continue believing in Christ, we need to step outside of secular classrooms, stop studying and listening to the news, and focus instead on what we know to be true in our hearts. If teachers call our students idiots for believing in creationism instead of evolutionism, then homeschooling is clearly a safer environment for Christians, right?

The thing is, if we believe God's Word is true, we can trust in the validity of our Creator. The Bible says that "The heavens declare the glory of God; the skies proclaim the work of His hands" (Ps. 19:1, NIV). Everything we see around us points us back to the Creator, so we never need to fear looking into a telescope or a microscope.

You can't bypass the mind in order to change your heart and life. Faith is not just about our feelings! In his book, *Serious Times*, James Emery White writes that "Jesus made it clear that our minds are integral to the life lived with God. When summarizing human devotion to God as involving heart, soul and strength, Jesus added mind."[9]

This is why it's so important for you as a Christian college student to do more than maintain your virtue and love to those around you. The church needs you to cultivate your mind. Apply yourself to your studies, whatever your major is. Broaden your horizons, deepen your understanding of the world, improve your memory and retention, develop critical reasoning techniques, and polish your writing and communication skills. These academic achievements will help you succeed in life and increase your effectiveness as a Christ-follower in our society.

You are the future, not only of our nation but of the church, and you need to be capable of defending the faith! As it says in 1 Peter 3:15: "Always be prepared to give an answer to everyone who asks you to give the reason for the hope that you have" (NIV). You need to study and get to the point where you believe the truth

The Truth, the Whole Truth, and Nothing but the Truth

wholeheartedly. Then you need to be able to explain why that belief makes sense.

Of course, I don't expect you all to study the Bible exclusively and become top-notch theologians. But the knowledge and wisdom you gain through studying the Bible will help you make better decisions in all areas of life. God has a unique calling for every person, and it's possible to honor Him as a scientist, teacher, business owner, or artist. The important thing is to commit yourself to do your best no matter what you major in. "Whatever you do, work at it with all your heart, as working for the Lord, not for men" (Col. 3:23, NIV).

God has more than an overarching purpose for your life. He has put you at this school for a reason, and He has a specific purpose for you today. Think about your goals and priorities. You came to college to learn, so learn! Please, don't give in to the current cultural epidemic of apathy. Find something you are passionate about and dive in! Just be careful to evaluate everything you're learning, both inside and outside of the classroom, based on God's truth, so that you can stand firm in what you believe. The years you spend in college are just like everything else in this life; they belong to Christ. Use them well.

4
LIVING IN HARMONY

Most people don't believe that I'm very shy, but it's true. With friends I'm loud and animated, often cracking jokes and prompting deep discussions with probing questions. But I have a hard time walking into a room full of strangers and striking up a conversation. In fact, I avoid events if I don't know anyone on the guest list. There is something about unfamiliar people and circumstances that scares me so badly, I mentally shut down.

When I moved into my first college dorm, the other students on my floor intimidated me. I wanted to make friends but was too scared to step out and introduce myself. So I devised a plan to make *them* come to *me*. I started a daily movie quotes quiz using the marker board on my door. The first person to guess the correct answer got an Oreo. I'm not proud of bribing my neighbors into talking to me, but it worked. I discovered that Kelsey, the red-haired advertising major from two doors down, shared my taste in movies. Years later, we are still friends.

Every new college student cares a lot about finding friends and fitting in. Outside of academics, relationships are the most significant part of college life. They greatly shape how you view yourself, your school, and your future. They also reflect how you're doing in your relationship with God and provide a powerful platform for evangelism. Therefore, the way you handle your various connections and how you treat those within your community deserves some serious thought.

Friends

Of course, one of the first things you want to do when settling into your new life at college is make some friends. Thankfully young college students have a multitude of places to find fellowship. First, befriend your roommate and the people who live nearby. Next, try to connect with your classmates and the people you work with. You can also join a sports team, club, or organization where you can get to know people who have similar interests. Church is a great place to meet friends! Never again will you find it this easy to connect with people of the same age and lifestyle. Take advantage of this incredible freedom while you've got it and spend time doing what you love with people you enjoy!

Just make sure that your new friends will exert a good influence and help you stay on track with your studies and spiritual walk. I liked the people in my dorm a lot, but they didn't share my values or work ethic. They stayed up late partying and playing video games instead of studying. If I had only hung out with them all the time, my grades would have really suffered. They also weren't interested in going to church. It was crucial to branch out and find Christian friends who would encourage me and hold me accountable.

Don't feel pressured to compromise your integrity or change your identity to fit in. Set boundaries and take care of yourself. You can easily find friends who will love and support the person you want to be. You might have to look beyond the first group of people you meet. But there are people on your campus looking for a friend like you!

We never really grow out of that desire to find acceptance and appreciation. In fact, I still feel that pressure, thanks to our lifestyle as a military family. My husband and I move around the world every two or three years, so it's very important for us to make friends quickly and establish a support network. That way we have people to turn to when we need something. It's like finding a substitute family while we're away from home. As a new college student, you will need to find a similar support network to help you through the next few years.

Living in Harmony

Family

Going to college marks a significant transition in your life. You're stepping into a new role in your family as you become an adult. Many of you are moving out of your parents' home and will be living on your own for the first time. Just as my husband and I have to figure out how to function without our immediate family each time we move, you'll need to think about how you're going to survive on your own.

The reality of how much I used to depend on my parents didn't sink in until a few months into my first semester away from home. I got sick and realized with dismay that I couldn't rely on them to drive me to the doctor, pick up my medicine, make me chicken noodle soup, or write a doctor's note to get me out of class anymore. I had to learn to take care of myself!

That revelation was tough. But for the most part, moving out was really fun. I enjoyed setting my own schedule and being free to make my own decisions. It's nice to have more control over your own life. Students often use their freedom to stay out late and do whatever they want without having to ask permission. But don't go overboard and get yourself into trouble. With great freedom comes great responsibility.

Your first year living on your own is a huge growth opportunity, and you should view it that way! True, it can be annoying to get yourself up for class, wash your own dishes, do your own laundry, prepare your own meals, and learn to pay bills. But these skills will help you succeed in life as an adult and—hopefully—as a spouse.

I remember some of my friends wanting to call their parents a week or two into the college term and thank them for everything they did to take care of them while they were growing up. During my first weeks away, I often needed something like paper towels or a measuring cup but didn't have it. It made me realize how many necessary items and comforts my parents provided back home. Taking that kind of selfless service for granted is more difficult when you learn what it takes to run a household.

Sometimes going to college gives the commandment to "honor thy father and mother" a whole new meaning. Suddenly all of their lectures come back to you, and as much as you hate to admit it, they actually knew what they were talking about! Don't be afraid to go to them for advice. Allow this to deepen your bond. As it says in Proverbs 1:8, "Listen, my son, to your father's instruction and do not forsake your mother's teaching."

College is a great time to get to know your parents better. Even if you weren't on good terms when you left, this could be a great time to work on those issues. Sometimes it's easier for relationships to flourish when you aren't living under the same roof. That was certainly true for my brother and me. We couldn't stand each other growing up but are now close. Time, space, and lots of prayer can heal many wounds.

Roommates

Speaking of the difficulty of living under one roof, the relationship with your roommate(s) will test your maturity and ability to love others selflessly from day one. How you all get along could make or break your college experience. So intentionally start this partnership out right. Whether you're moving in with a friend you've known since grade school or with a total stranger the housing office chose randomly, you'll learn a lot about each other in those first few days. Help the process along by being open, honest, and respectful of the other person's feelings when you encounter some differences. Talk through those issues and come up with a plan for sharing space that you both can live with and stick to it. Rooming with someone who grew up with different habits will take you some time to adjust to, but as long as you talk it through and are willing to compromise, you should be fine!

My relationship with my roommate could have been disastrous. She was older, smoked, and decorated her side of the room with red and black bedding and Slipknot posters. I'll never forget our first morning in the dorms. She habitually set her alarm clock a couple of hours earlier than she needed to and pushed the snooze button over and over. I'm often guilty of snoozing as well, but being jolted awake at the crack of dawn by blaring heavy metal music was not going to work for me. Clearly, we had some things to work out.

But beneath that hard exterior was a caring girl with a big heart for the Lord. It just took some effort to see the golden core beneath that hardened shell. We both grew a lot during that first year together. I learned how to be a self-sufficient adult. She quit smoking and made some other lifestyle changes to better honor God in her personal life. I don't know what I would have done during my first year away from home without my roommate. She became much more than another warm body taking up half of my space. She was a friend, confidant, and sister in Christ. The conversations we had while lying awake late at night were priceless. She had a different way of thinking and often called me out on things I needed to address when I started to backslide. I pray that you'll find a similar friend and advocate in your roommate.

Be vigilant in monitoring how you treat your roommate. The people you live with become your family at college. They're always around and see you at your best and worst. If you find yourself growing angry or resentful toward them, ask yourself why. The things that bother us most in other people often reflect the things we dislike about ourselves. They may reveal that you have some personal issues to deal with.

Romance

I bet romantic relationships are on your mind just as much as those with friends, family, and roommates. You're finally entering that time in life when you can start seriously searching for that special someone to settle down with. After leaving home and entering a new college community, you'll suddenly find hundreds of new fish in the sea. The subject of Christian dating is too broad to cover properly in this book, but it's extremely important! I strongly suggest you seek out other books on the subject and make sure you're prepared before jumping into that crazy social scene.

I will say, though, that in all your relationships and decisions during college, don't settle for anything less than God's best for you. He has a plan for your life. You may not be able to see where this narrow, winding path leads, but that doesn't mean He doesn't care about you or want you to be happy. Don't be tempted to pull over and find a more immediate solution to your emotional needs. God created love and romance. Don't buy into the enemy's lies and settle for what's quick and easy. The way of the world leads to shattered dreams, broken communities, and aching hearts, period. If you're feeling empty inside and overcome with longing, allow God to fill you up and trust in His promises. The love and appreciation of your future spouse will more than make up for what you think you're missing now.

As you wrestle with this issue, take some time to dig into God's Word. I think you'll discover that His rich, abundant love will more than meet your needs. "I pray that out of His glorious riches He may strengthen you with power through His Spirit in your inner being, so that Christ may dwell in your hearts through faith. And I pray that you, being rooted and established in love, may have power, together with all the saints, to grasp how wide and long and high and deep is the love of Christ, and to know this love that surpasses knowledge—that you may be filled to the measure of all the fullness of God" (Eph. 3:16-19, NIV).

FORGIVENESS AND LOVING LIKE CHRIST

Relationships are messy. While you're in college, God will push you to grow in your ability to forgive. Lessons could be small, like forgiving your roommate for eating your last packet of mac and cheese or forgiving your new friends for standing you up on Friday night. But God could also ask you to do something difficult, like forgiving your parents for past disappointment or abuse or forgiving someone you loved who betrayed you. As you get older and develop deeper and more serious relationships with family, friends, and romantic partners, your wounds may deepen as well.

Opening yourself up to new people can be scary. Whenever you choose to care about someone, you risk having your heart broken. The closer you become and the more you share the intimate details of your heart and mind with another person, the more it hurts when they reject you or break your trust. In a culture so riddled with sin and heartache, it often makes sense to become calloused and to avoid growing attached to people in order to survive. But God created us to live in community and wants us to exercise our tremendous ability to love.

As God said in Genesis 2:18, it's not good for us to be alone. Don't allow your heart to harden! That will not only keep you from making friends but also will prevent God from being able to work in your life. Running away from God will damage all your relationships and make life harder, not easier. Worldly relationships are marked by lies, cheating, gossip, and betrayal. But being open and loving in God's way produces joy and growth. Don't worry about what others think. Seek first the Kingdom of God, and He will take care of the rest (see Matt. 6:33).

One of the most difficult Christlike traits to develop is humility. Christians live in submission, which means we place our own needs and desires below those of others. We're called to do this for enemies and friends alike. Submitting to God and His ways is the key to living in harmony with others.

Viewing other people as broken souls whom God cares about, makes it easier to put aside our own wrongs and treat them with love and respect. As it says in Colossians 3:13, "Make allowance for each other's faults, and forgive anyone who offends you. Remember, the Lord forgave you, so you must forgive others." Scripture goes a step further than simply forgiving people once or twice and says we should be willing to forgive them hundreds of times (see Matt. 18:22). That's the way God works. He's slow to anger and rich in love (see Neh. 9:17). So next time your parents, roommate, or friends get on your nerves, view it as an opportunity for joy and growth. "For our present troubles are small and won't last very long. Yet they produce for us a glory that vastly outweighs them and will last forever!" (2 Cor. 4:17).

Learning to make wise choices about who to hang out with, how to build those relationships, and offering forgiveness rather than lashing out in anger will help you in the future as you get married or live with friends after college. God wants us to constantly grow in our ability to love others and to build a thriving community. All of these play a big part! One of my favorite Bible passages, which my husband and I used as our theme scripture at our wedding, serves as a great vision statement for your future role in the body of Christ:

> I pray that your love will overflow more and more, and that you will keep on growing in knowledge and understanding. For I want you to understand what really matters, so that you may live pure and blameless lives until the day of Christ's return. May you always be filled with the fruit of your salvation—the righteous character produced in your life by Jesus Christ—for this will bring much glory and praise to God.
>
> (Phil. 1:9-11)

Allowing our love for others to overflow from the Spirit's work in our hearts and growing in our understanding of what really matters in life not only helps us to have healthy relationships and succeed in college but brings glory to God. That is the ultimate goal of our lives. We're not just supposed to be happy and make a lot of money, we're supposed to be drawing others to Christ and honoring Him in all we do. As you think about your group of friends and how to strengthen your relationships, ask yourself if your love and joy in this group is contagious or if your group is exclusive and pushes people away from Christ.

Seeking Christ produces the fruit of the Spirit in your life (peace, patience, kindness, faithfulness, etc.) It's the thing that is lacking in nonbelievers and therefore makes you appealing. People who don't know Christ will see something different in you and wonder what it is and how they can get it. So share your life and the reason for your joy with everyone: not only friends and family but strangers and people you may not normally hang out with as well.

Outsiders and "Unlovable" People

Without a doubt, while in school you'll encounter people who are different from you. It's important to learn to love them, even if they seem to be completely unlovable. This is a big part of being a witness on campus! From Genesis to Revelation, the Bible is a story of God reaching out to the world through the lives of individuals. By making friends and building community, you are taking part in God's work in the world! "So all of us who have had that veil removed can see and reflect the glory of the Lord. And the Lord—who is the Spirit—makes us more and more like him as we are changed into his glorious image" (2 Cor. 3:18).

Of course, it's not always sunshine and rainbows. There are some people we just don't get along with. I'm not a confrontational person and often go out of my way to stay away from people who like to stir up drama or make me angry. We all have those people we avoid, maybe because they are annoying or make us uncomfortable. Or maybe it's worse. They could be a bully, a friend who stabbed you in the back, or an ex-boyfriend or girlfriend, and it just hurts to see them hanging out with someone new. It can be difficult to be nice to these people, let alone to like them or even love them.

The problem of dealing with these difficult people is nothing new. You'll face this challenge for the rest of your life. When sin entered the world after the Fall, our relationship with God and others fractured. We all experience lies, gossip, jealousy, hatred, pride, and betrayal. Thankfully, God doesn't leave us alone with our social troubles. Here is what Jesus had to say about the kind of person we should love.

> If you simply say hello to those who greet you, do you expect a medal? Any run-of-the-mill sinner does that… Now live like it… Live generously and graciously toward others, the way God lives toward you.
> (Matt. 5:43-48, MSG)

Pretty brutal, right? But it's true: we need to love everyone, not just those who love us back.

In Matthew 22, Jesus identifies the two most important commandments as loving the Lord with all your heart, soul, mind, and strength and loving your neighbor as yourself. Notice two things here.

First, God cares most that we always act out of love. We can't control our circumstances, but we can control our response. No matter what, we must love others as Christ loves them.

Second, Christ calls us to love our neighbor. Do we get to pick our neighbors? No. Jesus offers no qualifier that says we can stop loving our neighbors if we disagree or they hurt us. We still have to love them because He created them and wants us to love them as He loves them (and us).

It's too simple to say, "Love people because Jesus says so." It's hard to obey a command that feels unfair. You may be thinking: You wouldn't expect me to love these people if you knew what they put me through.

But think about this from His perspective. Jesus says to love others as He loves us. Do you think we're all that easy to love? Think about the way you treat God. Would He consider you to be a good friend?

Imagine that you gave up everything you cared about for your best friend who has made a commitment to love you and be devoted to you forever. But this friend barely talks to you and calls you only when he or she needs something. You overhear others badmouthing you, and your friend never sticks up for you but laughs and pretends not to know you. You watch every day as your friend wastes time and money on things you hate, barely having the consideration to apologize. Finally realizing his or her mistake, your friend makes an excuse and promises never to do it again. But you know it's only a matter of time before your friend slips up and betrays you once more. Would you put up with that? Talk about unlovable.

As it says in Romans 3:10, "No one is righteous—not even one." And yet in Psalm 103:8-12 we see that, "God is sheer mercy and grace; not easily angered, He's rich in love. He doesn't endlessly nag and scold, nor hold grudges forever. He doesn't treat us as our sins deserve, nor pay us back in full for our wrongs. As high as heaven is over the earth, so strong is His love to those who fear Him. And as far as sunrise is from sunset, He has separated us from our sins" (MSG).

Sin makes us truly unlovable. But Christ changed the rules when He died on the cross and offered us mercy and a relationship. How can we do anything less for others? It's especially important to grasp this idea of loving others as ourselves. If we're honest, no matter what others think about us, we've all felt unlovable from time to time.

Have you ever put yourself in other people's shoes and tried to figure out why they act the way they do? We all have our faults and quirks and make mistakes. But we all want to be loved and treated with respect. How can we judge others for something we're equally guilty of? "Sympathize with each other. Love each other as brothers and sisters. Be tenderhearted, and keep a humble attitude. Don't repay evil for evil. Don't retaliate with insults when people insult you. Instead, pay them back with a blessing. That is what God has called you to do, and He will bless you for it" (1 Pet. 3:8-9).

A Change of Heart

Changing the way we think and feel about people isn't easy—and it takes time. If you're having a hard time getting a grip on your emotions and loving difficult people, try serving them. Service is an action, not an emotion. Over time it'll help change the way you view those you serve. As you focus on their needs instead of their faults, you'll start to see them as people, not problems.

Serving starts with praying for them. You can also serve them by simply listening to them. Seeing that you genuinely care could seriously affect the way they think about themselves and treat others. That's what service does: it affects other people and helps build rather than fracture communities. As Richard Foster put it, "If a secret service is done on their behalf they are inspired to a deeper devotion.... It sends ripples of joy and celebration through a community of people."[1]

It takes integrity to be a good, godly friend who is caring and trustworthy. Set a goal to act the same way around every group of people you hang out with. Aim to put Christ at the center of your life all the time, not just on Sundays, because a person's true faith is demonstrated outside of church. If people see you as an honorable person, they're more likely to respect what you stand for and to listen to you when you share your faith. "Be careful to live properly among your unbelieving neighbors. Then even if they accuse you of doing wrong, they will see your honorable behavior, and they will give honor to God when He judges the world" (1 Pet. 2:12).

Despite our differences, God can work through every one of our relationships. Take the time to notice the people God has placed around you and pray that your relationships will help you both to grow. Be transparent and genuine in your friendships and build, rather than burn, bridges so that Christ can work through you inside your community.

Can you imagine what the world would be like if we took the gospel message seriously? What would your school or dorm be like if everyone went out of their way to love the wretched? How would the atmosphere change in the hallways if, instead of ignoring people or tearing them down with insults for things that they often can't help, we looked at people through God's eyes? What if we all forgave those who wronged us, even if they didn't deserve it? What if we took the reality of hell seriously and sacrificed our own pride and comfort to save the lives of the people we see every day?

It may sound crazy, but it's possible to make a big difference *today*. It starts with a few people making that commitment, right now. Be the change you want to see in your campus and in the world. Show them God is real, powerful, and full of love and mercy for all.

5
SET YOURSELF UP FOR SPIRITUAL SUCCESS

Have you ever tried to juggle?

It's a carnival trick that I've never mastered. The juggler begins by tossing two or three items in the air and moves them in an aerial loop by catching and throwing them in rhythm. If everything stays balanced and in motion, they add more and more items until they finally lose track and it all comes crashing down.

Between their studies, work, extracurricular activities, and relationships, students, these days, juggle too many things. With all that's riding on a complete college education, it's no wonder so many people turn to college self-help books for advice on how to survive. Every one of these college guidebooks emphasizes how important it is to set yourself up for success. Jam-packed with tips and tricks, they cover almost everything from developing good study habits, to writing an outstanding resume, to maintaining your desired weight while exclusively eating at the dining hall.

However, one aspect that is often conspicuously absent from these manuals is how to maintain a healthy spiritual life while getting a higher education. While it's important to pass your classes, many young Christians fail to realize that it's far more important to set yourself up to succeed spiritually. When life gets hectic and your to-do list starts to grow, spiritual practices are often the first thing to go. Without intentionally devoting time to your relationship with God, you will not be able to truly thrive in college—or in life.

A Life Way study[1] done in 2007 found that seven out of ten people who grew up in the church will walk away from their faith during college. I've known a handful of them myself, and it's heartbreaking. This statistic is especially alarming considering that today's college students will be tomorrow's leaders and shape our future. I don't think this happens because students suddenly decide to become atheists or to convert to a different religion. The process is gradual. The enemy is subtle. Persuasive lies can wear people down over time. Maintaining a healthy spiritual life takes a lot of work, and it's easy to let it slip when there are so many other things to worry about.

First-year students face special challenges as they adjust to living on their own in an unfamiliar place. Going out and finding a church can be intimidating, especially if they don't have a Christian friend to accompany them. New students quickly discover that it's difficult to get up early on a Sunday morning for church after a hectic week of classes and late-night fun on the weekend. Consequently, they may put that uncomfortable process off until a later date, assuming their faith is strong enough to survive without going to church for a while.

Like so many hopes and good intentions, the desire to find a church and continue living in obedience to God will fade unless you act and make it happen. Going to college is an all-consuming experience. Unless you decide early where and how you will spend your time and money, other people will quickly step in and decide for you. Homework will start to pile up after a couple of weeks. Finding the time and energy to pray and read your Bible after you've finished everything else will be difficult unless you make it a priority.

Also, the people you choose to hang out with will greatly determine how fruitful your spiritual life will be. If none of your friends has a relationship with Christ or feels a need to go to church, it's unlikely you will either. Don't get me wrong. The Bible says we're supposed to build relationships with Christians and non-Christians alike, but be careful whom you allow to influence you! Take these lifestyle choices seriously because the first few weeks of your college career will set you up for either spiritual success or spiritual stagnation.

Set Yourself up for Spiritual Success

You might ask why it's so important to find a Christian community like a church and to invest so much time into doing religious things. Isn't it enough to simply believe?

Technically, you don't have to go to church every week or practice spiritual disciplines, like reading your Bible regularly or praying, in order to be saved. We receive salvation by faith and not good works. But consider the following verse. "If you confess with your mouth that Jesus is Lord and believe in your heart that God raised Him from the dead, you will be saved. For it is by believing in your heart that you are made right with God, and it is by confessing with your mouth that you are saved" (Rom. 10:9-10).

Note that Paul lists two requirements for making ourselves right with God and being saved. We need to believe in the truth of the gospel, and we need to confess with our mouth that Jesus is our Lord. The second part about confessing with our mouth implies an outward action. When we say the prayer inviting Jesus into our hearts for the first time, we declare that we no longer want to be controlled by sin. As a result, we surrender the lordship of our life to Him. That means we have given up our selfish desires, and we have made our relationship with God the most important thing in our lives. The way we think, speak, act, and spend our time needs to reflect that change. Our obedience to our Lord shows our daily appreciation for this newfound freedom from the soul-crushing weight of our sin.

Don't go to church and spend time with God simply because someone says you're supposed to. That's the kind of reasoning you might expect from your parents. But the great thing about being a college student is freely thinking and choosing for yourself! This is one of the many reasons why I love college ministry. Once you make the choice to follow God wholeheartedly, incredible things start to happen in your life and the lives of the people around you!

This was definitely true in my case. Right after I graduated from high school, I underwent major back surgery to correct a severe case of scoliosis. The doctors told my family I'd need a full year to recover, which meant I had to stick around my hometown for my first year of college. I was disappointed because I couldn't wait to go to film school and learn how to make big, influential Hollywood blockbusters like *The Lord of the Rings*. Clearly God had other plans.

I spent my freshman year living at home with my parents and driving back and forth to the local community college. Those first few weeks were lonely, and I became depressed. As a social and ambitious person, I hated waiting to move on with my life. I needed community and support, badly.

It's hard to make friends on a commuter campus where no one hangs out before or after classes, so I decided to get involved in the college ministry at my church. To my surprise, I found more than a few friends through my membership in this group. Under the guidance of its inspiring leaders, I started to take my faith seriously and developed a passion for youth ministry. I also happened to meet the man I was going to marry!

I loved my life but hadn't given up on my dream to make movies. After my freshman year, I transferred to the College of Mass Communication and Media Arts at Southern Illinois University Carbondale. This transition was bittersweet. I was excited about getting back on track with my career goals, but I had to pack my bags, move a thousand miles away from home, and figure out how to survive on a big, secular college campus. Talk about intimidating!

My first two months at SIUC were miserable. I was homesick and missed my boyfriend. I abruptly encountered the ways of the world. I had a fairly sheltered childhood, so the drinking and partying overwhelmed and disgusted me. Thankfully, I had a great Christian roommate who kept me sane. However, she had a hectic work schedule. I spent many lonely weekends in my dorm room, writing to my friends back home and wondering if I had made the right decision to transfer out of state.

Adjusting to this huge change stressed me out. However, I started feeling a lot better when my roommate and I discovered InterVarsity Christian Fellowship, a group we had seen advertised on campus. Worshiping with a friend and hearing an encouraging message from God's Word was such a relief! I'm sorry to say I hadn't paid much attention to the Bible during that dark time. We signed up for a women's Bible study where I met fun people with similar values.

Then I asked around and found a good church in town that many of my new friends attended. I was also invited to a couple of retreats and conferences that challenged me and molded me into a stronger, more self-aware young woman. Eventually, I volunteered to serve on the leadership team and poured myself into helping other students discover this wonderful, transformative power of Christ.

I was a strong Christian when I left for college and would probably have kept my faith without getting involved in InterVarsity or a local church. But the support and accountability these ministries provided made my college years easier and more enjoyable. Everything I learned about God and myself, during those years, gave me a greater sense of purpose, which carried me through all the crazy ups and downs of college life. The opportunity to serve and positively influence others allowed me to walk away from college with more than just a diploma. By becoming a member of this thriving community of believers, I made awesome, lifelong friendships—which is what every college student wants. I changed for the better and gained valuable life experiences that I never would have achieved by exclusively focusing on my degree.

This kind of life-altering spiritual growth requires you to step out of your comfort zone and to pursue God in a big way. As we saw in the Romans passage earlier, God wants us to take action! Don't worry. You don't have to do this on your own. You can find the encouragement and guidance you need to get started in four places. These resources are available to all college students and can help you succeed spiritually.

THE CHURCH

Too often people tell me they love and believe in Jesus Christ but hate the church. When they say they hate the church, what they probably mean is that they've lost faith in the imperfect human institution we call the church. For most of us, church refers to the building, worship services, and Sunday school classes we attended every week, growing up. We think of it as a specific location or group of people. But the church of the Bible is bigger and simpler than that. Jesus and His disciples defined the church as the entire body of believers who followed Him. As it says in Ephesians, "Instead, we will speak the truth in love, growing in every way more and more like Christ, who is the head of his body, the church. He makes the whole body fit together perfectly. As each part does its own special work, it helps the other parts grow, so that the whole body is healthy and growing and full of love" (Eph. 4:15-16).

The church is the heart of Jesus Christ. He loves this group of believers as a groom loves his bride on his wedding day, with an all-consuming joy and desperate desire for her happiness and well-being. In fact, He loved the church (and by extension, us) so much that He was willing to die a gruesome death to ensure its survival. All that Jesus said and did while He was here on earth purposely built up this body. Truly loving Jesus yet hating the church seems impossible to me. That would be like telling your best friend you love him but hate his wife. Can you really love someone if you reject the biggest and best part of him or her?

Maybe we struggle with attending church because we're self-centered and believe the church exists purely for our benefit. Everything, from the way the minister speaks, to the type of music that is played during worship, to the size of the congregation and the way people interact with each other, needs to be just right. Otherwise, we dismiss it as a poor fit and search for a church that better suits our needs.

This kind of attitude creates multiple problems. First, it keeps us focused on ourselves and what we want rather than on God and what He wants. As it says in the Ephesians passage above, we should try to become more and more like Christ, loving people as He loves us and working together as a united body of believers. Focusing on our own needs and desires makes this almost impossible.

Second, there's no such thing as a perfect church. If you keep switching churches until you find one with no problems, you'll never stay in one place long enough to experience the wonderful blessing a church can be. Even though God established the church and infused it with His Spirit, the people who attend are broken and make lots of mistakes. But that's the beauty of it! The church community consists of all kinds of people who come to the cross fully aware of their sinful nature and work together to bring glory to God. Churches come in all varieties, and each one offers something different. What matters most is that you find the time in your busy schedule to gather with your fellow believers and to worship our Lord and Savior.

Many people's past experiences with the church have hurt them, so remember that the church consists of broken, sinful individuals. Even if you haven't yet been offended, neglected, or otherwise scarred by the people in your church, you might be in the future. When you enter a church and make yourself vulnerable while searching for acceptance and redemption, you could be devastated to find rejection and judgment instead. While you've heard that Jesus Christ loves everyone, you may find that people who call themselves Christians will turn you out for wearing the wrong shirt. Or for asking a question. Or for supporting the wrong political candidate. Or for expressing a different opinion, let alone for your true faults and mistakes. Once you've been burned by one church, you may find it difficult to try again. Why should you open yourself up to people who are only going to judge and reject you? Why would you want anything to do with a God whose followers are cruel hypocrites?

This is why we should look at Christ and not at the church. He is perfect, and we are not. "If we claim we have no sin, we are only fooling ourselves and not living in the truth. But if we confess our sins to Him, He is faithful and just to forgive us our sins and to cleanse us from all wickedness" (1 John 1:8-9). Just as God forgave us when we didn't deserve it, we need to work on forgiving the people from our past who have hurt us. Remember, the church is an institution and can't harm you. The body of Christ didn't inflict this pain on you and doesn't need your forgiveness. But His people do. We believe we're all saved the same way: through the undeserved shedding of His blood on the cross. He doesn't want anything to prevent anyone from experiencing the fullness of His grace and love. Only when we can forgive and start to love those who have wounded us will we truly begin to heal. As Peter writes,

> All of you should be of one mind. Sympathize with each other. Love each other as brothers and sisters. Be tenderhearted, and keep a humble attitude. Don't repay evil for

> evil. Don't retaliate with insults when people insult you. Instead, pay them back with a blessing. That is what God has called you to do, and he will grant you his blessing.
>
> (1 Pet. 3:8-9)

The church is a place where broken people come together and learn what love truly is. The sooner you allow God to work on your heart through His Word and His body, the better.

College only lasts for a brief time. However, many habits you develop during this period will continue throughout the rest of your life. Finding a church and attending regularly while in college will make it easier to do so later in life. If you only participate in a college Bible study or youth group, you may still be spiritually healthy. But after you graduate, you'll be completely on your own! Just as your classes are designed to help you build skills for your future career, your participation in a church will help equip you for your future in the kingdom of God.

You may think, "Yeah, I understand that going to church is important, but you have no idea how busy I am! I don't even have time to sleep, let alone spend an entire morning in church!" Believe me, I've been there. My senior year in college, I was balancing a full course load, all my InterVarsity leadership responsibilities (which totaled about six to ten hours a week), writing and producing my senior thesis film, maintaining a long-distance relationship, and planning my wedding while being a thousand miles away from home! Even with all that, I managed to have a thriving spiritual and social life while keeping my grades up. Trust me, you can do it! Time-management skills and a healthy perspective will keep you focused on what's most important.

I'll never forget a sermon I heard at my home church in Colorado during my freshman year. The college minister based his lesson on Luke 4 where Jesus is teaching in the synagogue. He pointed out that we accept without question the fact that Jesus went to the temple. He was raised as a Jew after all. But He must have found it very tedious and tiring. If anyone in history had the right to say He wasn't getting anything out of a sermon or had more important things to do, it would be the Son of God Himself. Yet He considered

Set Yourself up for Spiritual Success

it a worthwhile use of His time, if only to walk among people and serve them with His gifts.

Do you need a good reason to drag yourself out of bed on a Sunday morning and go to church? Here's one: The church needs your gifts. God gave you a specific set of spiritual gifts so you will use them. Paul says in 1 Corinthians 12:7, "A spiritual gift is given to each of us so we can help each other." As a young Christian, you have the energy and talent to do big things for God. You can serve the church in many ways, from playing or singing in the worship band to leading a Bible study, joining a prayer team, or volunteering with the youth program and setting a good example for younger kids. God can use your passions to build His kingdom on earth.

Not only will the members of your church and your community benefit from your fellowship and assistance, but you will as well! You'll be challenged to do things you never imagined you could do—things that require you to stop relying on your own strength and to trust in God. Consequently, you'll experience tremendous personal and spiritual growth. Also, as you work closely with the other people in your church, you'll start to develop incredible friendships that will make your time in college more enjoyable and will continue for years after you graduate. Some of the most meaningful relationships I made during college were with older people at my church. They were mentors and friends I could go to for help or advice while I was away from home. But the best part about getting involved in a church is experiencing the deep, life-affirming satisfaction that comes from serving the Lord with all your heart.

If you are unsure of how to get started or are having a hard time finding a good local church, a great place to go for help is a parachurch organization, like a college ministry or a youth group.

College Ministry

Parachurch organizations such as InterVarsity Christian Fellowship, Campus Crusade for Christ, and the Navigators exist to help students discover and develop their gifts so they can use them to build the church. The encouragement and personal training these groups offer enable you to make the most out of your spiritual endeavors.

Many churches don't train students in ministry or provide leadership experience. But college ministries offer all kinds of opportunities to try new things and serve as leaders. Many people who have been heavily involved in a parachurch organization go on to be significant leaders in their future churches.

College ministries offer much more than assistance in building your religious resume. When you're involved in a church, you get to interact and worship with all kinds of people. But in a college group you experience close fellowship with people your own age, sharing in the joys and hardships of college life.

Because churches need to appeal to a wide variety of people, some of the topics they cover on Sunday mornings may not interest you as a young student. But within a college ministry, you'll hear sermons catered to you and what you're going through right now. The people who speak during these meetings have worked with a lot of young adults and know the spiritual challenges you face on a daily basis. For example, in a typical church service you might hear about things like marriage, parenting, and finances, which are all important. But your campus minister will probably focus more on things he or she knows you need to hear such as what the Bible has to say about peer pressure, fleeing from sexual immorality, and discovering God's will for your future. These messages are geared to help you grow in your faith and generally as a person.

Hearing this extra bit of teaching each week will give you a more Christ-centered perspective that will hopefully keep you on track as you go about your daily life on campus. It's not easy to live for Christ while in college. So many worldly influences, temptations, and distractions can prevent you from doing what you know is right. Getting involved in a community of believers will help you become the person God created you to be.

Your parachurch organization will also equip you and give you opportunities to testify about the difference Christ has made in your life. Witnessing to your friends and classmates can sometimes seem like an insurmountable task. You may feel like no one wants to hear you talk about your faith—and even if they did, you wouldn't know how to begin! Even though I grew up in a church, I never received any training on the subject. I know many others are in the same boat. But campus ministries exist to help students minister to the campus! Most of them hold several outreach events throughout the year where you can share your faith and serve the community. Working within a larger group and doing service projects with people you know allows you to start stepping out of your comfort zone instead of feeling pressured to plunge in by yourself.

Remember, a college ministry is more than a social club. You go to learn about and worship our Lord and Savior. While you attend your weekly meetings or are out on service projects, focus on more than having fun with your specific group of friends. Reach out to new people and outsiders. Prove that God loves and embraces *everyone*! Your living example might lead someone to salvation!

Bible Studies

The most influential program your church and/or college ministry offers is their network of small-group Bible studies. The single greatest thing you can do to succeed spiritually in college is joining one of these groups. While you can hear wonderful, applicable sermons in your church or college group, that's not the best forum to ask questions or discuss how the text applies to you. In a small group Bible study, you have a chance to dig into the Word with a group of believers and figure out what it really means. As you wrestle with these issues, you'll get to know each other on a deeper level and build incredible friendships based on honesty and trust.

Having solid Christian friends to hang out with, talk to, and rely on in a time of need makes a big difference. Being a college student devoted to Christ isn't easy. As a new undergrad, you will go through a rapid intellectual and emotional growth spurt. By stepping out into the world on your own, you begin the process of defining who you are and where you're headed. Meanwhile, all kinds of people and organizations will try to influence you and draw you into their way of living and thinking. This can be overwhelming, and the voices you listen to most will begin to shape your thinking and actions.

Sharing the journey with people who knew and spoke the truth helped me a lot. Not only did they provide the accountability I needed to stay on track, but they loved me for who I was rather than using my companionship for their own benefit. Your relationships often determine how you feel about yourself and the whole college experience, so seek out a great college ministry where you can find this kind of life-affirming friendship!

DISCIPLESHIP

One of the strongest and longest-lasting types of Christian friendships develops through discipleship. What is discipleship? It's a simple idea that Jesus put into practice while He was here on earth. A disciple studies under or follows another person—just as Peter, James, and John were disciples of Christ. So discipleship is essentially Christian mentorship.

Within the traditional model of discipleship, a more mature believer connects with a person of the same gender who is younger in his or her faith. They meet periodically to study the Bible, talk about life, and pray for one another. An important part of this relationship involves holding each other accountable for taking steps of faith toward positive change. Because these meetings focus exclusively on your needs, they provide an opportunity to dig in and work on areas where you're struggling. Then you do the same for your partner. Over time, you help each other become the best versions of yourselves. Consequently, people who invest in this discipline often grow into compelling Christ-followers who are rock-solid in their faith and are passionate about spreading the Good News.

The way Christ discipled people in the Bible is the ideal means to establish church leadership and draw people into the circle of believers. Jesus chose a few friends whom He challenged to walk with Him, learn from Him, and emulate His ways. As Jeffrey Arnold explains, "He asked questions of them, taught them, admonished them, prodded them to take steps of faith, nurtured them and loved them."[2] When the disciples had matured spiritually, He sent them out into the world to share the Gospel and make disciples of others— who would do the same.

Paul illustrates the process of making disciples in 2 Timothy 2:2. "And the things you have heard me say in the presence of many witnesses entrust to reliable men who will also be qualified to teach others" (NIV). If a church or community invests in guiding and equipping young believers, the number of wise, gifted, and willing Christian leaders will grow exponentially—all the greater for extending God's kingdom!

Christians who are serious about growing personally and spiritually will benefit from discipleship, which involves becoming a follower as well as a believer. Following requires action. Beware: discipleship is not for the faint of heart! At its core, it's a quest for greater obedience, which is the key to fruitfulness.

Thriving means to be fruitful. Consider what it says in the book of Psalms: "Oh, the joys of those who do not follow the advice of the wicked, or stand around with sinners, or join in with mockers. But they delight in the law of the LORD, meditating on it day and night. They are like trees planted along the riverbank, bearing fruit each season. Their leaves never wither, and they prosper in all they do" (Ps. 1:1-3).

When we obey, we have a clear conscience and uninterrupted fellowship with the Lord. First we must deal with all the sinful thoughts and tendencies holding us back. It's not easy. It's a process. But it certainly helps having a friend along for the ride whom you trust and respect. As long as you're willing to open yourself up to self-examination, to be humble and honest with your partner, and to practice what you learn, incredible things are possible.

Many churches and youth groups encourage discipleship and can set you up with a mentor. Even if they don't have an established organization devoted to discipleship, you can always approach someone you trust and ask if he or she would be interested in meeting with you. There is more than one way to go about this. You can come up with your own system as long as you're committed to honoring God in all you do.

I suggest you spend the first couple of weeks simply talking and getting to know one another better. Remember, your discipleship partner is supposed to become a great friend! Then pick a topic or a book of the Bible to read together and discuss how it applies to your life right now. Commit to acting on what you discover so you'll grow and change for the better. Expect to meet God along the way because I'm confident He's planned something big and exciting for you! As it says in Philippians 1:6, "There has never been the slightest doubt in my mind that the God who started this great work in you would keep at it and bring it to a flourishing finish on the very day Christ Jesus appears" (MSG).

Think back to the passage from 2 Timothy where Paul talked about disciples entrusting the gospel message to reliable men and preparing them to teach others. Discipleship is a two-way street. Its purpose is to equip you to make disciples of others. The ideal model of discipleship within a youth group involves people being discipled and discipling others at the same time. When Christ gave the great commission, He called us to continually invest in the lives of others, bringing each new generation into relationship with Him (see Acts 1:6-8). The process must begin anew with us. As you're learning and growing and beginning to achieve spiritual success, don't forget to pay it forward!

I firmly believe that God has placed you at your school for a reason. Your purpose at any time in life is to reach out to everyone you encounter and share the love of Christ with them. But this is especially true in college when you have a chance to meet and build relationships with so many different people. It's unlikely you'll ever have a larger circle of influence than you do right now, so take advantage of this incredible opportunity!

College ministries have the ability to significantly shape the lives of young people. But students can't benefit from this blessing unless they are willing to allow God to work in and through them. So pay it forward! If you feel you've benefitted from being involved in any of the Christian communities discussed in this chapter, share your story with others and encourage them to take the next step toward spiritual success. Imagine the difference you could make as a senior if you took a few freshmen under your wing and helped them get plugged into the ministry! They have four years ahead of them in which God can mold them into powerful and effective witnesses—think of the possibilities!

Set Yourself up for Spiritual Success

During my senior year, I met a freshman girl named Leann at church. She hadn't found a niche yet, so I invited her to InterVarsity. She lived nearby and started attending the Bible study I led in my dorm. I saw potential in her, so I asked if she would be interested in meeting with me for discipleship. Even though she was three years younger, we shared the same spiritual passion and soon became close friends. After I graduated, she took over my leadership position in InterVarsity and later became the chapter president. Since then, she's worked as a church intern and has participated in several major mission trips to the Dominican Republic, Haiti, and Southeast Asia. She now continues to live as a sold-out Christian. I can't take any credit for her journey—that's all God's power and providence. But I know she's done remarkable things through this campus ministry. I'm humbled to think that she's had these opportunities because God nudged me to invite the new girl to join us.

By taking a few minutes out of your day to encourage a young believer, you could unknowingly help to bless several people that person serves later in life. Remember that nothing you do for God is worthless. As it says in 1 Corinthians, "So, my dear brothers and sisters, be strong and immovable. Always work enthusiastically for the Lord, for you know that nothing you do for the Lord is ever useless" (1 Cor. 15:58). By being faithful to God in a small way now, you will be helping to fulfill the big plans He has in the world!

6
FROM THE INSIDE OUT

Before we can go out into the world and inspire great change, we need to look inward. God has clearly stated that He cares most about what goes on inside of us. "It's who you are and the way you live that count before God. Your worship must engage your spirit in the pursuit of truth. That's the kind of people the Father is looking out for: those who are simply and honestly *themselves* before Him in their worship" (John 4:23-24, MSG). The key to thriving and living life to the fullest is giving Him access to your inner life so He can transform you from the inside out.

God has given us several tools to help us on our journey to inner reformation called spiritual disciplines. These practices give God access to your life so you can slowly let go of all the sinful things that hinder you spiritually and steadily mature in your knowledge of and relationship with Christ. In Richard Foster's acclaimed book, *Celebration of Discipline*, he offers this introduction, "The classical disciplines of the spiritual life call us to move beyond surface living into the depths. They invite us to explore the inner caverns of the spiritual realm [and] urge us to be the answer to a hollow world."[1]

I always assumed that spiritual disciplines were associated with older, more traditional religious practices, and didn't find them very exciting. But Foster reveals that they speak to the struggles of our generation. When he sent the book to the publisher over thirty years ago, he wrote this in his cover letter, "This book is for all those who are disillusioned with the superficialities of modern culture, including modern religious culture."[2]

He's making two big claims here. First, our superficial, shallow culture can't provide lasting happiness or fulfillment. This is an important lesson for new college students to learn early in the year. When you arrive at school, you'll be free to partake of all the world has to offer, both good and bad. If you settle for the norm—hanging around your dorm doing nothing, going to class only when you feel like it, eating nothing but mac and cheese, ramen, and pizza, and saving up your money so you can get sloshed every weekend, you'll most likely walk away from college feeling you've got little to show for your four-year investment. No. Foster claims (and I agree) that if you want to find real happiness in your life, you need to dive deeper into the Spirit.

His second claim is harder to swallow. Foster implies a lot of modern religious culture is just as superficial as secular culture. In other words, simply going to church and pretending to be a good Christian won't cut it. Growing up, you may have discovered that many Sunday school classes, churches, and popular fads held little meaning for you. For example, did you ever stop to ponder what Jesus would have done in a particular situation when you were wearing your WWJD bracelet? I know I didn't.

Instead of embracing contemporary ideas of spirituality, we should look to Scripture and the people throughout history who developed a deep and transforming relationship with God. The "disciplines" our Christian forefathers practiced can help you achieve the deep, inner peace that you've heard about but may not have experienced. It's great because anyone can practice these spiritual disciplines at any time. You don't have to possess substantial, theological knowledge to attempt them. They provide a way for people to deepen and enrich their relationship with God on a daily basis. Don't feel overwhelmed when reading through the extensive lists of spiritual disciplines. Even trying to implement one at a time will help you grow closer to the Lord.

Learning to be self-disciplined and overcoming bad habits that limit your growth will help you in all aspects of your college career. The following spiritual disciplines highlight how following God's calling can significantly improve your life.

Bible Study

As you're pursuing a higher education, you'll need to read and study a lot to succeed in your classes. It may not always be fun, but hitting the books will pay off when your grades are posted. Regardless of how much you care about academic achievement, there is one book you *should* commit to read and study daily. It's the "Good Book," better known as the Bible. God has been transforming lives and teaching people to thrive through the written Word for centuries. If you want to truly understand yourself, your origins, and your place in the world, you need a working knowledge of the Creator.

Our God values communication. More than anything, He desires to develop a relationship with us, and that requires getting to know each other. That's why He gave us His Word. It's a tangible way for Him to speak directly into our lives.

Some people think the Bible is merely a religious text, something that contains history lessons or moral guidelines. I admit that I grew up thinking that way. I believed the Bible was the most important book in the world, but it was still just a book. Over the years, I've discovered that I can read the same verse over and over but get something new out of it every time. The Bible really is the living Word, infused with the Holy Spirit and able to provide the wisdom you need. God understands what is going on in your life. If you seek Him through Scripture, He'll reveal the truth about who He is, any sin that needs to be dealt with, and how to find lasting joy and satisfaction. "Every part of Scripture is God-breathed and useful one way or another—showing us truth, exposing our rebellion, correcting our mistakes, training us to live God's way" (2 Tim. 3:16, MSG).

Jesus is the perfect example of someone who loved God's Word. "He used scripture to answer those who tested Him, resist temptation, find guidance, encourage His heart, comfort others, explain His actions and ultimately face His own death."[3] Christ proved that Scripture contains the wisdom we need to live well. We should learn all He has to teach us so that we'll be equipped to follow in His footsteps. God calls us to be obedient and to meditate on His word every day, not because He wants us to behave but because He cares about who we'll become. He has revealed the secret to fulfilling our purpose, and it's all found within those pages.

The trick is knowing how to comprehend and apply what you read. The Bible may be God-breathed and a wonderful way to grow closer to Him, but it was written thousands of years ago and is not what you'd call an easy read. Its stories are about people from ancient cultures who have long names like Nebuchadnezzar and Artaxerxes that are hard to pronounce let alone to remember. Books like Leviticus and Numbers record the Jewish laws and genealogies, which can be tedious and boring to read straight through. But don't get discouraged! Personal Bible study tools and methods can help you make sense of Scripture. Learning to read the Bible successfully is a lifelong process; like any other skill, it takes time and practice to master.

First, find a Bible translation you can easily understand. Some people grew up reading the King James Version, but all of the *thees* and *thous* can be hard to sift through. I was raised with the New International Version, which is a good middle ground between a literal translation of the original text and modern language. But there are many others out there.

When I finally committed to reading through the Bible on my own, I thought it would help to have one I picked myself instead of the Bible I won in third grade for reciting memory verses. Something about the pride of ownership made picking it up more appealing. So I chose three or four passages throughout the Bible I knew fairly well (for example, Genesis 1:1, John 3:16, and Psalm 1). Then I went to a Christian bookstore and read through those verses in several translations until I found one that spoke to me. I ended up purchasing the New Living Translation, a well-recognized version with a style that's more accessible for young people. The Message may also be a good option for those trying to read through the Bible for the first time. As a paraphrase, instead of a word-for-word translation, it sums up the gospel in modern-day terms so it's easy to read and understand.

While you're looking at Bibles, you may want to look for a study Bible that includes tools such as maps, a concordance, and footnotes explaining the context and meaning of words. You can purchase these resources separately if you've already got a Bible you like. Use the Internet if you find something that confuses you. Printed and online commentaries by biblical scholars provide rich insights to help you understand what you're reading. You can even look up passages of Scripture in different translations online to compare the wording. There are also all kinds of Bible apps loaded with daily reading plans, devotionals, and study tools so you are never without God's Word!

As you start reading, you can organize your thoughts and let the message sink in by using a variety of tools. I have a method of personal Bible study I use on a daily basis and highly recommend to others. My friends and I call it SOAP, which stands for: Scripture, Observation, Application, and Prayer. It's easy! Sit down and read a little bit of the Bible every day and record these four things in a notebook or a journal. First, look for the verse or verses that jump out at you for any reason and write them down. This is your daily scripture. Then write out your observations: What is the author saying? Rewrite the verse in your own words to make sure you understand it. Next, reflect on how the verse applies to your life right now. What do you need to do or change based on what God has revealed? Finally, write out a short prayer asking for God's help. The goal of SOAP (as with all Bible study) is a life change. No matter what part of the Bible you read, you'll be amazed how God reveals exactly what you need to hear.

The artist method[4] may help those who are more visual than verbal. As you read, draw one of three things. When you run across something that speaks to your heart, draw a little heart in the margin. (Yes, it is perfectly OK to write in your Bible! Do anything that helps you get closer to God!) Whenever a new thought or idea strikes you, draw a light bulb. Finally, if the scripture is moving you to do something, draw a hand and write what action you need to take. Feel free to underline, highlight, or draw arrows that help you process what you are reading.

For those who are audio learners, *lectio divina* may help you pull greater meaning from scripture. *Lectio divina* simply means "holy reading,"[5] and it's a way of attending to God's Word, which people have been using for centuries. It calls you to slow down and sit with the words you read, praying over them and allowing God to speak through them and touch your heart. Traditionally, *lectio divina* has four parts. First, clear your head and focus on God. When you're ready, read a passage of the Bible out loud several times, lingering over words so that they sink in. Write down the ones that stick out. Next, meditate on the verses. Reflect on the importance of the words that catch your attention. What is God trying to tell you? After that, respond through prayer. Read back through it again, but this time, enter into a personal dialogue with God. How does the message make you feel? Where are you resistant or unsure? Finally, sit back and rest in the presence of God. Let it all sink in and surrender to the Lord. Allow His love and peace to fill you up as you go about your day!

Memorizing specific verses you find encouraging or challenging will strengthen your relationship with Christ. As you study your Bible, write down those key verses on a note card and tape it to your mirror or above your desk—somewhere you will see it often. Then as you go about your daily routine, God can continue to speak to you, guiding your thoughts back to Him. Our culture no longer values memorization, but you will greatly benefit from training your mind to hold on to important information. If you lock God's truth away in your mind and write it on your heart, you'll never be without it when the need arises. As it says in the Psalms, "I seek you with all my heart; do not let me stray from your commands. I have hidden your word in my heart that I might not sin against you" (Ps. 119:10-11, NIV).

As with all new skills, repetition is the key. Familiarize yourself with scripture and the resources I mentioned, and your understanding will increase as you get more out of your devotions. The more you read God's truth, the more you will live it out. Just be sure your heart is in the right place. The goal is not to simply know more but to know God. We come to scripture to be changed. For that to happen, we need to be humble and willing to learn. It can be hard work, and your pride may take a few hits. But just like studying for your classes, the effort is completely worth it! The greater hold you give God over your heart and mind, the more you will begin to experience His love, joy, peace, patience, kindness, goodness, faithfulness, gentleness, and self-control in your everyday life (see Gal. 5:22-23).

Prayer

Through prayer, you can make the jump from knowing what the Bible says to knowing God personally. More than anything, God desires to build a relationship with you. Bonding with God is similar to the way you connect with your other friends. Talk to Him! Listen to what He says. Get to know Him and learn to trust Him. Then you can share your joys and sorrows with Him and invite Him in to make a difference in your life. This interaction builds your faith because it moves you from simply reading that God is real to seeing it with your own eyes and personally experiencing His power and grace.

Prayer is the instrument God uses to change us for the better. To grow closer to Him, we need to talk to Him about everything that is going on in our minds and hearts. Yes, *everything*. Remember, He already knows it all anyway. So why not take off the mask and step into the light? Give Him the good, the bad, and the ugly and ask Him to heal the hurts and make you stronger. Giving up control and admitting how you've sinned can be hard. But the great news is that God loves you and wants the best for you. You don't need to hide from Him anymore.

Unfortunately, our prayer life can suffer the same way our social skills do. I can't tell you how many awkward encounters I've had in the last twenty years and how many people I've hurt or ignored without even realizing it. How much more do we hurt God with our short, infrequent, whiny prayers? He created us and proved how much He loves us by sending His son to die on a cross to save us. Doesn't He deserve more time and attention than even our best friends? Prayer should be more than a small habit we practice when we feel like it. Building intimacy with the Lord is a spiritual discipline that should take top priority in our lives.

Jesus believed prayer was incredibly important. He got up early and went off on His own to talk with His father and to be refreshed and energized for the day ahead (see Mark 1:35). The disciples recognized the quality of His relationship with God and knew it had something to do with His prayer life. So they asked Him how to pray. He taught them The Lord's Prayer, which believers recite in church services across the world. Jesus prayed, "Our Father in heaven, hallowed be Your name. Your kingdom come. Your will be done on earth as it is in heaven. Give us day by day our daily bread. And forgive us our sins, for we also forgive everyone who is indebted to us. And do not lead us into temptation, but deliver us from the evil one" (Luke 11:2-4, NKJV).

Jesus tells us that when we pray we should first recognize God's sovereignty and surrender to His will. Then we can ask Him for our basic needs, for forgiveness, and protection from temptation. This is a great model for anyone who lacks experience with prayer and struggles to know what to say. Following Jesus' example is always a good way to go.

Another method, abbreviated ACTS, might help. It stands for: Adoration, Confession, Thanksgiving, and Supplication. Begin by praising God for who He is. Look to scripture for inspiration while highlighting His characteristics. The Psalms are full of His praises! This step is important because it expresses your love and respect for God and keeps your prayer focused on your relationship, not on what you want Him to do. Next, confess the sins and weaknesses that separate you from God and ask for His forgiveness and healing. We know He will faithfully forgive us and remove "our sins as far from us as the east is from the west" (Ps. 103:12). No matter how severe the crime or how deep the stain, He can make us as clean and pure as fresh fallen snow (see Isa. 1:18). Consequently, we need to thank Him for His incredible love, mercy, and provision. Finally, supplication means to ask for what you need. Tell Him what is going on in your life and in the world around you and request that He intervene and make it right.

Your prayers don't need to be formal or complicated to be effective. What matters is where your heart is. Be authentic. Come to God as you are and open yourself up to His direction. Sometimes you don't even need words. Simply sitting still and delighting in the presence of the Almighty, works wonders. Because He understands the human condition so well, the Lord has provided a way to pray when you feel like you're drowning in sorrow and don't know how to ask for help. If you cry out to God, the Holy Spirit will intercede and convey the feelings you can't express (see Rom. 8:26).

As you grow closer to God, He will begin to reshape your world view. The more you read God's Word and ask Him to direct your paths, the more you will begin to see everything from His perspective. Suddenly, the worldly things that seemed so essential before, no longer appeal to you. The problems that scared or overwhelmed you before, pale in comparison to our glorious God. He will teach you to see people through His eyes, and you will learn to love and serve them unconditionally. Through prayer, God will mold you into the best possible version of yourself and give you the strength and encouragement to make it through anything.

Many people have a hard time believing that God wants us to pray big prayers. They're afraid to bother Him with their problems. But Jesus clearly states that He wants to hear from us and delights in answering! In fact, our lack of imagination probably disappoints Him. He has the power to do exactly what needs to be done in the world right now, but He chooses to use ordinary people to accomplish those extraordinary things instead. God put us here to mature through challenges and to prove to skeptics that He is real, by doing the impossible through His power! Christ is just waiting for us to step up to the plate.

The spiritual heavyweights in the Bible all prayed expecting God to answer in a big way. They knew He was listening and had the power to grant their requests. They also prayed as if their prayers would make a difference. Abraham prayed boldly that God would change His mind and spare the cities of Sodom and Gomorrah if He could find a few righteous people living there. Moses had to intercede for the sinful Israelites, time and time again. When King Hezekiah fell ill and Isaiah the prophet told him he was about to die, Hezekiah called out to the Lord in prayer. Because he was a faithful servant, God was merciful and said, "I have heard your prayer and seen your tears. I will heal you" (2 Kings 20:5). The Bible tells us that the prayers of a righteous person are powerful and effective (see James 5:16). So we should take this discipline seriously and start praying for the needs around our campus and the world.

It is important, though, that our requests be rooted in God's character. He is completely good and just and will not grant a request He knows is wrong. In addition, He is all knowing and concerned with a much bigger picture than we could ever comprehend. He knows what needs to happen in the world, and sometimes the way He chooses to bring it about isn't easy for the people involved. We may pray for something we believe God wants—healing, for example—and it doesn't happen. At this point, many people struggle and falter in their walk. Why didn't God answer their prayers? How could He let this happen? What was He thinking? God doesn't need to explain Himself to us, but to those who ask such questions He offers this reminder: "My thoughts are nothing like your thoughts.... And my ways are far beyond anything you could imagine. For just as the heavens are higher than the earth, so my ways are higher than your ways and my thoughts are higher than your thoughts" (Isa. 55:8-9). All we can do is trust in God's goodness. He may not always answer our prayers the way we want or expect, but He promises to always be with us, love us, and comfort us no matter what.

Service

We have dwelt quite a bit on what Jesus said is the greatest commandment of all: to love the Lord your God with all your heart, soul, mind, and strength. Reading your Bible and praying are ways to seek Him out and build that relationship. But Jesus goes on to say there is another equally important commandment, to "Love your neighbor as yourself" (Mark 12:31). The spiritual discipline of service puts that commandment into action on a daily basis.

Service involves more than just a list of things you do to help others. It includes walking the talk and living out what you claim to believe. A big part of becoming a servant is beginning to think the way God does. He wants you to really pay attention to the people around you and to work with Him to meet their needs and heal their hurts. Many people on your campus have never read the Bible or gone to church. So watching you may be the only way they will learn who Jesus is. Help them see and feel His grace and love in action!

Show them you really care. All through the Bible, God uses ordinary people to reach the nations. It's the same today as it was thousands of years ago. God wants to send you out into the world to be His hands and feet.

Americans find this is tough because most of us work our whole lives to get to a point where we can quit serving others and be served instead. We want the good life, free from worry and burdens. Few of us aspire to remain at the bottom of the totem pole. Jesus' disciples acted in a similar way. They often bickered about which one of them was the greatest and which one of them was the least. But Jesus says that to become truly great we must serve (see Matt. 20:26). He values leadership and authority but redefined what they require.

In biblical times, everyone walked around in sandals or was barefoot. After a day of traveling, mud and dust covered their feet. So it was customary for someone to wash their feet before they sat down to dinner. As you can imagine, no one would want this dirty, smelly job. Only the lowest, least important person in a group got stuck with that job. Usually it was a servant of the host who was responsible for washing feet. But one night when the disciples stopped for a meal, Jesus shocked them all by getting down on the floor and washing their feet. Then He said, "Now that I, your Lord and Teacher, have washed your feet, you also should wash one another's feet. I have set you an example that you should do as I have done for you" (John 13:14-15, NIV).

Jesus demonstrated what it means to serve others. He sacrificed His own comfort and dignity to show these men how much He loved them. He considered their needs to be just as important, if not more so, as His own. This is the Christlike attitude we need to strive for. Service makes us reevaluate our own self-importance. As Jesus demonstrated, no one is too good or too busy to do even the most basic service.

It may not be easy to put your own needs and desires aside to help someone, especially if you get little to no credit for it. But as you selflessly serve others, you will grow more humble. God calls us to control the sinful desires of the flesh, meaning any of our natural human passions (sex, money, fame, etc.). If we don't, we'll continue to rely on our own power instead of learning to depend on God. Pride gets in the way of our relationship with the Lord.

Humility is an important trait for all college students to develop. It makes you teachable and increases your compassion for others, which will deepen and enhance your relationships. As you attend to the needs of others, you will begin to experience a new joy and love for Christ. Therefore, service is a spiritual discipline that will benefit everybody.

Be careful that your priorities are in the right place. There is a difference between self-righteous service and true, selfless service. Self-righteous service is motivated by the desire to get recognized for doing something big in the world. People who think this way only serve when they feel like it or when it's required. They pick and choose whom to serve because they are concerned with results and hope those people will be able to pay them back in kind. It's like giving a Christmas gift to manipulate someone into buying one for you. But true servants reach out and commit acts of kindness even when they don't feel like it. A lifestyle of service flows from their love for God. They're drawn to small, often overlooked tasks that are just as important as contributing to major charities. True servants don't exclude anyone from their ministry. Where needs arise, hands raise up to meet them. They are content to remain hidden. The only opinion that matters to them is the Lord's.

If you're unsure which of these two categories you fit into, try this exercise. Divide a piece of paper into three columns. Label column one "For Me," column two "For Others," and column three "For God." Then list in each column all the things you've done or spent money on in the last month for that category. What does this reveal about the state of your heart? Are you loving your neighbors as much as yourself?

Sometimes Jesus' call to serve can be intimidating. This is one of the spiritual disciplines that I struggled with the most in college. As a naturally fearful person, I was uncomfortable stepping outside of my comfort zone and doing something that might affect what people thought of me. I also believed that in order to serve others I had to take a lot of time to do something big, like visiting a nursing home or going on a mission trip. Those are definitely great ways to bless your community, especially if you go with other believers. But service doesn't need to be grand or complicated. Start small, and Jesus will teach you how to expand your efforts. Look for areas around your school that need attention and people within your sphere of influence who could use a little extra care.

You can serve humbly and stand up for those who normally get made fun of or exploited by listening to them and encouraging them. Take care of basic needs whether you are thanked or not. Give a neighbor a ride or straighten up the common area of your dorm. Serve others in loving hospitality. You don't have to make it a big production. It's just a chance to get together with friends in a safe place and to celebrate. Performing these small acts of service helps you get to know God by applying His Word in the world around you. Serving also gives you an opportunity to build relationships and develop your spiritual gifts.

The biggest part of serving in love, however, is witnessing to those around you about the free gift of salvation that Christ offers. He commanded us, "Therefore, go and make disciples of all nations, baptizing them in the name of the Father and the Son and the Holy Spirit" (Matt. 28:19). So many college students need to know Jesus. He has intentionally placed you where you are to help Him reach the lost and hurting on your campus. He created us to do this, so we should remove anything standing in our way. As Bruce Wilkinson put it, "God loves you infinitely and wants you in His presence every moment, and if He knows that heaven is a much better place for you, why has He left you here on earth?"[6]

You don't have to earn a master's degree in theology to share your faith. Even brand new believers have a story to share. Anyone can pray and serve and bring glory to God in the process. As Martin Luther King Jr. said, "Everybody can be great because anybody can serve. You don't have to have a college degree to serve. . . . You only need a heart full of grace, a soul generated by love." I challenge you to start praying for God to bring someone into your life whom you can serve.

Rest

Do you sleep enough at night? Are you able to relax during the week and find time for yourself? I kept myself busy all day, every day, while I was in college and would have answered a resounding, "No," to both of those questions.

I've learned from experience that resting and slowing down are essential spiritual disciplines and help maintain a healthy relationship with God and everyone else. My InterVarsity staff worker emphasized rest because he had seen how destructive burning the candle at both ends could be for college students physically, emotionally, and spiritually.

Workaholism and sleep deprivation present big problems in today's society, especially on college campuses where students live at full throttle. You're expected to carry a full course load, a job, be involved in various clubs and activities, work out periodically, and enjoy a social life on top of that. Under this constant pressure to succeed, it's hard to justify taking time to relax and recuperate. You don't have to look far to see how workaholism compromises our health and relationships.

We have limits, and that's not a bad thing! Adele Ahlberg Calhoun says in *The Spiritual Disciplines Handbook*, "Rest can be a spiritual act—a truly human act of submission to, and dependence on, God who watches over all things as we rest."[7] Whether we believe it or not, we have enough time every day for all that God requires of us, including rest. Resting reminds us that our identity in Christ matters more than how much we accomplish in the world. You won't get to your future any faster if you hurry, and rushing definitely won't make you a better person. The more you overextend yourself, the less you become.

The author of Ecclesiastes wrestled with this concept. He tried everything he could think of to find fulfillment on this earth, including work and the achievement of great riches. But in the end he reflects, "So what do people get in this life for all their hard work and anxiety? Their days of labor are filled with pain and grief; even at night their minds cannot rest. It is all meaningless" (Eccles. 2:22-23). Jesus also knew that rushing around and working all the time was futile and pointed people to what really mattered: a relationship with Him.

The story of Mary and Martha comes to mind. Over the years, teachers have used it to demonstrate where our priorities should lie. Luke 10:38-42 reads:

> As Jesus and the disciples continued on their way to Jerusalem, they came to a village where a woman named Martha welcomed him into their home. Her sister, Mary, sat at the Lord's feet, listening to what He taught. But Martha was distracted by the big dinner she was preparing. She came to Jesus and said, "Lord, doesn't it seem unfair to you that my sister just sits here while I do all the work? Tell her to come and help me." But the Lord said to her, "My dear Martha, you are worried and upset over all these details! There is only one thing worth being concerned about. Mary has discovered it, and it will not be taken away from her."

When we slow down and take time to rest, we not only recover physically but find time to reflect, pray, and regain a proper perspective on life. Slowing down gives us an opportunity to look at Christ instead of only seeing the items on our massive to-do list. Teaching ourselves to slow down isn't easy, especially when much of our schedule is already planned for us. Here are some practical things to help us get started.

First, ask yourself this question: Is your alternative to work, more work?[8] Learn to set a goal for the day, and once you've accomplished it, do something fun or take a nap. I knew a fellow college student who refused to hang out with people because she insisted she had too much work to do. As a result, her relationships really suffered. Graduating was an unpleasant shock, and she regretted not enjoying the college experience while she had the opportunity. Don't let that be you! Work when you need to and use your remaining time to rest, to be with God, or to go out and make some memories!

Second, go on a retreat. The atmosphere on a college campus often makes it difficult to rest or have quality time alone. There are always people around, and it's always noisy. It's hard to relax in a dorm room, even if you manage to have it to yourself for a while. I've told my husband that I refuse to set up a work space in the same room where we sleep or entertain guests. I learned early on in college that it's almost impossible to sleep while staring at the work piled up on your desk. Conversely, it takes a great deal of motivation to work when your bed is calling to you from across the room.

To find peace and give yourself an opportunity to unwind, you need to get outside of your normal routine and away from the hustle and bustle. Go outside, take a walk, read in a local park, or take a day trip with friends to explore the area. Maybe it means going over to a friend's apartment to watch a movie instead of doing so on your laptop. Take your Bible to a coffee shop and devote an afternoon to catching up with God. Take naps! Take advantage of retreats through your church or college ministry plans where you really get to leave everything behind. Do whatever it takes to make space in your life for God!

Finally, if you have a hard time slowing down, you may need to unplug for a while, which brings us to our next discipline.

Fasting

We often misunderstand fasting and see it only as the act of going without food for a period of time. While this is somewhat true, it completely misses the point of the discipline. Fasting isn't the physical act of not eating. It's a spiritual practice and should only be done for spiritual reasons. When you fast, you take the time you'd otherwise devote to acts of self-indulgence, like eating, and use it instead to pray or meditate on God's Word. You're not punishing your body to earn favor with God. You're eliminating distractions that prevent you from having a deep and fulfilling relationship with Him.

Salvation doesn't require fasting, but Jesus practiced and encouraged it. He fasted for forty days before beginning His ministry and continued to fast and pray regularly until His crucifixion. Since the Son of God considered it important to fast, it will benefit us spiritually. However, His idea of how and why we should fast differed greatly from the views of His contemporaries. Unlike the Pharisees, who used fasting as an outward sign of piety, Jesus defines it as a private, spiritual discipline that is seen only by God:

> "And when you fast, don't make it obvious, as the hypocrites do, for they try to look miserable and disheveled so people will admire them for their fasting. I tell you the truth, that is the only reward they will ever get. But when you fast, comb your hair and wash your face. Then no one will notice that you are fasting, except your Father, who knows what you do in private. And your Father, who sees everything, will reward you."
> (Matt. 6:16-18)

I've known about fasting but had no desire to practice it until recently. I like to eat and figured there were better ways to demonstrate that I trust God to provide for me. However, as I've been reading about all the spiritual disciplines, I have run across a quote that that completely changed my perspective. It's not about food; it's about learning to live without the material things we're attached to and depending on Christ for our fulfillment instead. Foster says in *Celebration of Discipline*, "More than any other discipline, fasting reveals the things that control us . . . [it] helps us keep our balance in life. How easily we begin to allow non-essentials to take precedence in our lives. How quickly we crave the things we do not need until we are enslaved by them!"[9]

You can certainly fast in the traditional sense by abstaining from food for a period of time. For more information on how to do that safely, consult credible resources on the subject. For me, the deeper issue here is identifying the things that distract college students and hinder their spiritual and personal growth.

Self-indulgent distractions saturate the modern college experience. Because you're no longer under your parents' control, you do whatever you want, whenever you want, no matter what. You're going to college to get an education, but you live in an environment that makes it difficult to get anything done. If your dorm room resembles the one I lived in, you sit in front of your computer all day, are constantly texting, the TV is always on, your music clashes with your neighbor's, and your open door allows people to step in and interrupt you at any time. (I won't even begin to discuss what happens when alcohol gets thrown into the mix.) You're expected to study, rest, and pray in an environment like that?

If you want to enjoy a positive experience in college and cultivate a thriving relationship with Christ, you have to find a way to shut out the noise and pay attention to what really matters. It's not that difficult to do if you convince yourself you don't need the stuff you've been turning to for comfort or amusement. *The Spiritual Disciplines Handbook* defines a fast as "the self-denial of normal necessities in order to intentionally attend to God in prayer. Bringing attachments and cravings to the surface opens a place for prayer. The physical awareness of emptiness is the reminder to turn to Jesus who alone can satisfy."[10]

It disturbs me that people of our generation can go for days without praying or reading their Bibles but can't last a few hours without their cell phones or Internet access. How do you spend your time? Are you more devoted to Jesus Christ or Mark Zuckerberg, who founded Facebook?

Take some time to think seriously about the worldly things you depend on for security or satisfaction or that needlessly eat up a lot of your time. Here is a list to consider:

Email	Social Media Sites
Chatting Online	Watching Internet Videos
Video Games	TV
Cell Phones/Texting	Eating
Shopping	Partying

I challenge you to give up one of those things for a day and use that time to read your Bible or pray. It won't be easy. You'll probably get fidgety, anxious, or bored if you can't text or play with your gaming system. But in the end, you'll be amazed at the difference it makes. Not only will your mood and your sense of spiritual well-being significantly improve, but you'll probably be much more productive in your studies. When you can't connect with people through technology you might be motivated to actually leave your room and spend time with them face to face. What a concept! God wants us to thrive and develop intimate relationships with others, but we can't do that until we let go of things that distract us from glorifying Him.

Celebration

College students can easily get wrapped up in negative thoughts. Think about your recent conversations with friends. When you ask someone how they are, do they often respond by grumbling about being tired, busy, or bored? The Bible teaches that what you focus on most will truly affect your attitude. If you only think about your monstrous to-do list, the annoying things your roommate does, or how much you hate walking to class in the cold, your outlook will be pretty bleak. But if you remember to keep all the good things in your life at the forefront of your mind, you'll enjoy your college experience so much more! That's why I've chosen celebration as my final spiritual discipline.

What do you do when your team wins the big game?[11] You scream, jump up and down, and exchange high fives and fist bumps. Some furniture might get damaged in the process, and you will relive those final seconds in conversation for weeks to come. Girls, what do you do when he finally asks you out? Do you immediately call or text your friends to share the good news? How long do you wait before changing your relationship status on Facebook? Our culture knows how to celebrate when something exciting happens. Why do we have such a hard time publicly celebrating what matters most: our relationship with God?

Celebration and joy lie at the heart of the way of Christ. He entered the world amid great celebration. "I bring you good news of great joy that will be for all the people" (Luke 2:10, NIV). Before He ascended into heaven, He passed on His joy to the disciples. "I have told you these things so that you will be filled with my joy. Yes, your joy will overflow!" (John 15:11). Joy and celebration in our lives stem from a deep love of God and His creation. Truly knowing God leads us to passionately and publicly praise Him. Eugene Peterson says,

"The Bible's smiles carry more meaning than its sermons."[12] Have you found this to be true in your life?

More often the opposite is true. I found the university I attended was particularly apathetic. While I was there, InterVarsity put together a huge outreach called Justice Week, where we tried to raise awareness about human trafficking and the illegal sex trade. Exploring a controversial topic could provide a platform to discuss issues like justice, truth, and faith. But few students were even willing to stop and talk to us for a couple of minutes between classes about something so outrageous. They didn't get fired up; they didn't even seem interested in learning more or sharing their opinion.

I attended the vigil the school organized for the victims of the Virginia Tech shooting in April 2007. This tragedy affected a lot of people, and we all talked about it in the dorms and during classes. But on a campus of more than 20,000 students, only 150 people showed up. Many of them were staff members or from the local community.

I even knew many people who were not excited about their major. How do you get by on a daily basis, going to class and doing homework, if you don't like what you're studying? Joy produces energy and gives us the strength to make it through anything that gets thrown our way. How do you survive, let alone thrive, without it?

Joy is the result of a right relationship with Christ. If our attempts to follow in His footsteps don't bring us joy, something may be wrong. If we're more focused on what we're doing than on what He has done for us, our misuse of the spiritual disciplines may become a stumbling block in our spiritual walk. Instead of helping us to know Christ better, the disciplines can become rigid laws we must follow to please God. People with this mindset have stepped into the tricky world of religious legalism and cease to grow spiritually because they believe they already know what needs to be done to earn God's grace. The disciplines of the spiritual life are not laws, and whether or not you practice them has no bearing on your salvation. They are simply ways to express your love for God and to live in obedience to His will.

From the Inside Out

Too many of us make daily choices that lead to unhappiness. We rationalize the sin in our lives and choose to live according to the world's rules. Then we go to church on Sunday to seek a miracle fix for the emptiness inside. But God desires to transform our misery, not magically erase it. If we live in continual obedience to God, we experience more and more of the freedom from anxiety and discontent that He offers. Joy refreshes our spirit as the disciplines function in our lives.

Learning to celebrate takes a lifetime. We have to work at it and return to it when life gets rough. As a military spouse, it is all too easy to feel like a victim. Moving every few years and holding down the fort while my husband works twelve-hour days or deploys to faraway places creates an emotional and spiritual burden. Many wives leave family, friends, and careers behind to follow their husbands all over the world. Loving and supporting our nation's defenders is an important calling. But sometimes the sacrifice of our personal comfort and dreams becomes too painful and leads to bitterness and depression.

I was tempted to join the cranky-wives club when I got married. What a transition: graduating from college, leaving all of my friends in Illinois, packing up my room at home in Colorado, getting married, and moving to a small border town in Texas where my husband was finishing his pilot training. I panicked as I faced growing up, seemingly overnight. I had to put my dreams of being a Hollywood filmmaker on hold indefinitely. I knew God had a plan and that my husband was worth the sacrifice. But in moments of weakness I struggled to see the good in my new situation.

Thankfully, my mother-in-law bought me a wonderful book that helped change my perspective called, *Cold Tangerines: Celebrating the Extraordinary Nature of Everyday Life,* by Shauna Niequist. The author uses stories from her life that illustrate how God works through even our most mundane moments. She spoke to me in the midst of my pessimism and self-pity. In the introduction, Niequist writes:

> I know that the world is several versions of mad right now. I know that pessimism and grimness sometimes seem like the only responsible choices. . . . And that's why I'm making a shameless appeal for celebration. . . . The discipline

> of celebration is changing my life, and it is because of the profound discoveries that this way of living affords to me that I invite you into the same practice. . . . What God does in the tiny corners of our day-to-day lives is stunning and gorgeous and headline-making, but we have a bad habit of saving the headlines for the grotesque and scary. . . . To choose to celebrate in the world we live in right now might seem irresponsible. . . . But I believe it is a serious undertaking, and one that has the potential to return us to our best selves, to deliver us back to the men and women God created us to be, people who choose to see the best, believe the best, yearn for the best.[13]

This book taught me how bad I am at thanking God for all of His blessings. My ungrateful attitude not only brought me down but also hurt my husband and friends as well. So I have made the conscious choice to celebrate. I even started a blog to help remind me to look for the little, exciting, and beautiful things that God is doing in my life. I may still struggle to keep smiling amidst the hardships of the path God has set before me, but the more I rely on Him for my joy and fulfillment, the better life gets!

I encourage you to do the same! When you notice that you're frustrated, bored, or depressed, take some time to note all the little things you have or do that make you happy. If you can't think of anything, that probably means you need to spend some more quality time with God. He has blessed us with a life full of joy and beauty, which will come into sharp focus if we keep our eyes on the Creator and not our own junk.

> And now, dear brothers and sisters, one final thing. Fix your thoughts on what is true, and honorable, and right, and pure, and lovely, and admirable. Think about things that are excellent and worthy of praise. Keep putting into practice all you learned and received from me—everything you heard from me and saw me doing. Then the God of peace will be with you.
>
> (Phil. 4:8-9)

7
WHEN IT RAINS...

It pours. I'm still convinced all my professors got together and scheduled our major tests and projects at the same time. I expected that during finals, but it seemed to happen repeatedly throughout the semester too. My busiest weeks coincided with major extracurricular activities and holidays, making it doubly hard to be productive. In addition, my body rebelled at the worst times, and I got sick. Tears often fell as I attempted to muscle my way through a haze of sleep deprivation and decongestants. Add to that any kind of relationship crisis, and I was sure to spiral downward into a major meltdown. With a lot of prayer, perseverance, and chocolate, I managed to make it through with my grades and friendships intact. But I always knew anxiety would bubble up again.

College students ride an emotional roller coaster full of highs and lows. Many struggle to maintain control during these turbulent years. It's not only stress that can cause problems. As you step out on your own and become an adult, you will face many trials and tribulations. One minute you're enjoying life and the next you feel like your world is crashing down around you. Living up to expectations and doing the right thing while still having fun and sleeping is a balancing act worthy of Barnum and Bailey. It can take all that you've got just to hang on until graduation. How do you thrive under these conditions?

Accepting the fact that you'll go through tough times and committing to face them with a positive attitude is half the battle. Jesus didn't sugarcoat the truth about the difficulties of life. Sometimes it just sucks.

We live in a broken world full of pain and suffering. Bad things often happen to good people who don't deserve them. This is true for believers and non-believers alike. But Christians have God to help them through it. As Jesus said, "I have told you all this so that you may have peace in Me. Here on earth you will have many trials and sorrows. But take heart, because I have overcome the world" (John 16:33).

Attitude plays a key role. When things take a turn for the worst, how do you react? Do you rely on God and cling to His promise to help you through it, or do you fall to pieces? As you may have guessed, I tend to fall into the second category. I'm a passionate person with a big imagination—a combination that can be a blessing and a curse. When I'm in tune with God, I don't allow anything to stand in my way. But my moods shift rapidly, and my lows are as forceful as my highs.

Emotions are good; God gave them to us for a reason. He created us in His image and gave us the ability to feel as He does. Scripture describes God as being joyful, sad, compassionate, angry, and jealous for our love and loyalty. In the book of Psalms, God laughs! Our emotions help us connect with God and others. However, we can't let them control us or prevent us from doing the right thing. Feelings change constantly like shifting sand. But we need to build our faith on the Rock so that when the winds of change and uncertainty blow, we will be secure (see Matt. 7:24-27).

Studying God's promises and believing the truth in the Bible strengthens our faith. When we know God is completely benevolent and just and always acts for our good, it's easier to trust Him no matter what happens. As it says in Psalm 91:1-4, "Those who live in the shelter of the Most High will find rest in the shadow of the Almighty. This I declare about the LORD: He alone is my refuge, my place of safety; He is my God, and I trust Him. For He will rescue you from every trap and protect you from deadly disease. . . . His faithful promises are your armor and protection."

When It Rains…

Learn to make the best of your hardships while in college rather than giving in to despair and anger. God gave you emotions, and what you do with them matters. He doesn't waste any experience in our lives but uses them all to shape and mold us into the men and women He created us to be. Stay alert to how He's working in every circumstance.

When we lose everything, we're left with nothing but God and each other. Sometimes that's a good thing. Realizing that we're not in control and need help to survive drives us back into God's arms where we belong. These tough seasons help keep things in perspective and motivate us to focus on what matters most.

My husband's first operational assignment in the Air Force took us to Misawa Air Base in northern Japan. God definitely used this move to test our faith in His goodness and intentions. Leaving our family and friends behind thrust us far outside of our comfort zone, and we had to learn to rely on Him completely for our security and emotional well-being.

Our new home placed us only 150 miles north of the epicenter of the catastrophic earthquake and tsunami that struck Japan in March 2011. The disaster left us scared and stressed. Fortunately, the worst effects we experienced were being violently tossed around and losing power for a few days. But for weeks afterward, a continual stream of intense aftershocks rocked us, leaving us constantly on edge, wondering if another monster quake was headed our way. When the power returned, we watched the news in horror as footage of the destruction down south flooded in. We watched images of giant boats and trucks being tossed around like toys in the surge of the tsunami. Satellite footage revealed miles of blank coastline where entire towns had been swept away. Add to that the reports about the rising danger from a damaged nuclear plant, and we couldn't help but wonder why? Why would God allow this to happen?

This question often creates a major roadblock in our ability to believe in and trust God. Human beings have struggled with the idea of evil and suffering in the world for ages. How can an all-powerful, completely good God allow innocent people to suffer?

But God didn't give us death and suffering; we invited them into the world when we chose to disobey Him and believe the devil's lies instead. The fact that evil bothers us should point us back to the Creator, not push us away from Him. If there is no God and we are all intrinsically good creatures who've developed in the most natural way, we shouldn't have a problem with reality.[1] If the weak and poor suffer and die, it's due to natural selection, not to tragedy. If the earth shakes and the mountains fall into the sea, that's just the way the universe works, and we have no right to complain. But because we're created in the image of a righteous and loving God who planted the vision of heaven in our souls, we naturally recognize and abhor injustice and cruelty.

By sending Jesus to die on the cross to save us from our sins and giving us the Holy Spirit to guide us in our renewed relationship with Him, God provides us with the strength and ability to wage war on the corrupt ways of the world. If we're wondering why nothing has changed and people still suffer needlessly, I think God has the right to ask us the same question.

Too often we grow narrow-minded and allow our past hurts or fears of the future to cripple us so we fail to see God working in the present. This topic inspired the bestselling novel *The Shack*, which tells the story of a man who faces a tragedy no one should ever endure: losing a child to kidnapping and abuse. As the main character wrestles with his pain and fears, God asks this simple question that cuts me to the core, "Do you realize that your imagination of the future, which is almost always dictated by fear of some kind, rarely, if ever, pictures Me there with you?"[2]

God tells us not to be afraid 366 times in the Bible. "Fear not, for I have redeemed you; I have summoned you by name; you are mine. When you pass through the waters, I will be with you.... When you walk through the fire, you will not be burned" (Isaiah 43:1-2, NIV). He is our shield, our fortress, an ever-present help in trouble (see Ps. 46). He will never put us in a situation we can't handle.

The heart of fear lies in our failure to trust God. If we completely trust God's goodness and judgment, we have no cause to fear. Evil still exists in the world whether we have faith or not. But as

When It Rains…

Frederick Buechner put it, "The Psalmist doesn't try to explain evil. He doesn't try to minimize evil. He simply says he will not fear evil."[3]

You need to fear God more than you fear what He's called you to do! After all, there is only so much a person can do to hurt you here on earth. But your spiritual health has eternal consequences. "Do not be afraid of those who kill the body but cannot kill the soul. Rather, be afraid of the One who can destroy both soul and body in hell" (Matt. 10:28, NIV).

When we come up against something we fear, it trips our default switch, and we start to backslide. It's never good to move backward in your walk with God; you want to make progress. When you face trials and temptations, you should spend even more time in prayer! Learn to go to God first, not to people who might lead you even further astray. When you're in crisis, you'll hear a lot of voices giving you unbiblical advice. Learn to discern God's voice!

When we dwell too much on our hurts or mistakes, they begin to define us. That's not what God wants for your life. Will you allow the crisis to be an excuse or will it become a part of your testimony? Will you choose to focus on how hard things are or on how God always gives you the strength you need to survive? For "we are pressed on every side by troubles, but we are not crushed. We are perplexed, but not driven to despair. We are hunted down, but never abandoned by God. We get knocked down, but we are not destroyed" (2 Cor. 4:8-9).

When I feel my anxiety rise, remembering that fear often amounts to nothing more than my "False Expectations About Reality" helps me keep things in perspective. I fear the unknown. With my overactive imagination, I tend to dwell on the worst-case scenario and lose sleep picturing all of the terrible things that might happen. "Can any one of you by worrying add a single hour to your life?" (Matt. 6:27, NIV). If you are prone to worry like I am, it might help to copy this acronym for FEAR (False Expectations About Reality) onto an index card and stick it on your bulletin board or mirror.

God has a bigger perspective than we do, and we need to train our brain to think the way He does. We need to admit that we're just a small piece of the humanity puzzle, a single thread in the tapestry of history, and one pixel in the bigger picture of what's going on in the world. We may never know why things happen the way they do, but we can trust that God is working, slowly leading us all down the path He has chosen.

Take the earthquake and tsunami in Japan for example. It's hard to understand why God would allow that to happen. I don't believe He wanted those people to suffer and die. However, God has used this tragedy for good. It forced the proud Japanese people to accept outside help, knowing full well they could never repay their benefactors. Humbling themselves enough to accept a free gift helped them grasp previously foreign concepts at the core of Christian doctrine. Communities that were once permanently closed to missionaries started welcoming their message of hope and grace. The Holy Spirit opened the doors to western religion, once more, and is actively saving souls that would otherwise have been lost. I went on multiple mission trips down the coast after the tsunami and got to witness this redemption first hand. We couldn't help but rejoice in the midst of our sorrow—thanking God for the mysterious way He works to save His people.

God has given us a powerful weapon against pain and fear: hope. This isn't just an empty wish, like saying we hope it won't rain tomorrow. No, the biblical definition of hope is blessed assurance: the expectation that He will fulfill His promises no matter what. The Lord has given us a peek at the final chapter, and we know that good *will* triumph. This knowledge should help us live with great confidence. No matter how dark or bleak things may seem right now, we know it doesn't matter. As long as we believe that Jesus Christ is our Lord and Savior, the story of our life will end happily ever after in heaven.

Horatio Gates Spafford took this lesson to heart and continues to inspire suffering souls everywhere. A successful lawyer, he lived with his wife and five children in Chicago in the late 1800s.[4] Unfortunately, the family suffered a great tragedy when their only son passed away. While they were still grieving, the Great Chicago Fire of 1871 ruined Spafford financially. A couple of years later, he and his family decided to travel to England to visit his friend Dwight

When It Rains...

L. Moody. Spafford was delayed on urgent business but sent his wife and daughters on ahead of him. On November 22, 1873, their ship sank, and all four girls drowned, along with 222 other souls. When his wife reached England she sent him a telegram that read "Saved alone."

As Spafford made the crossing to join her, the ship's captain let him know when they reached the site of the sinking. As the story goes, he went below deck and penned the words to one of the world's most beloved hymns, "It is Well with My Soul." Here are some of the lyrics that helped get me through the pain of my back operation, all the fear and uncertainty surrounding my husband's military career, and the traumatic events following the earthquake in Japan. May you find solace in their truth as well.

> When peace like a river attendeth my way,
> When sorrows like sea billows roll,
> Whatever my lot, thou hast taught me to say
> It is well; it is well with my soul.
> Tho Satan should buffet, tho trials should come,
> Let this blessed assurance control
> That Christ has regarded my helpless estate
> And hath shed His own blood for my soul.

We always want to be happy, healthy, and comfortable. But the sin that runs rampant in the world makes that impossible. God doesn't promise to take away all our pain and suffering, but He does promise never to abandon us. We can experience peace and contentment in our relationship with Him until we join Him in heaven. He definitely possesses the power to fix all our problems, but often He allows them so we'll draw near to Him, develop spiritual and emotional endurance to help us fulfill our calling, and learn to depend on Him rather than on our own strength and ability.

The hard truth is that our faith can't grow apart from trials. Just as strong winds force trees and plants to send down deeper roots in order to survive, resistance and difficulties will deepen your spiritual roots. When you ask God to grow your faith, you invite Him to put you into an uncomfortable place. Instead of complaining and reverting back to old habit patterns, embrace this opportunity to better yourself and fight your way through. "When troubles come your way, consider it an opportunity for great joy. For you know that when your faith is tested, your endurance has a chance to grow. So let it grow, for when your endurance is fully developed, you will be perfect and complete, needing nothing" (James 1:2-4).

Sometimes God has to break into our lives and separate us from the familiar so we'll pay attention to Him. If God wants to teach you something, He'll put you in a hard spot. Pain calls new parts of our minds, emotions, and bodies into action, like sending blood flowing back through a numb limb. At first it hurts, and you feel like you've got pins and needles jabbing you all over. But to have feeling is a good thing; it means you're alive and able to move again!

Spiritually speaking: no pain, no gain! When we work out, we accept that we'll get sore for a while before we build up our strength. Why are we willing to accept physical pain in order to grow but not emotional or spiritual pain? Don't allow your fears and problems to incapacitate you. Instead, build up a little spiritual muscle so you can accomplish great things in the future! "They [Bible heroes] weren't great because they were fearless but because they acted in faith in spite of their fears."[5]

Remember that no one can follow God and be comfortable for long. But you can trust Him to fulfill His promises if you remain faithful. If you can endure until the end, He will bless you.

The last chapter discussed the discipline of celebration. It's difficult to celebrate and give thanks to God when our lives fall apart. But that's when it's most important to praise Him. When you feel like you're stuck in a valley and can't climb out, make a list of all the things you're thankful for. You'll be surprised to discover how richly He's blessed you, even in the worst of times.

8
Taming Temptation

As a follower of Christ, you're already better able to handle the twists and turns that being in college brings. Christians understand the difficulties of life and the ugliness of sin better than the rest of the world because they see it in their own lives and understand why it's there.

But not all bad things you encounter in college are a test from God. Trials and temptations are very different. Trials are difficult times God uses to strengthen you. But He never tempts you to do the wrong thing. Evil is contrary to His nature, and He's incapable of producing it. Tough consequences result when we deviate from God's will. Thankfully, redemption is possible after making a poor choice. He can still work in your life and help you grow after you repent. But the repercussions of sin are not a part of His plan for you, so it's best to avoid it from the start.

On a college campus, you're surrounded by more sin than you can imagine. Beyond the obvious vices of excessive drinking, drugs, and sex, college students (like most other people) indulge in pride, greed, laziness, jealousy, and gossip. Even people with a good Christian upbringing are tempted to compromise or dabble in things that seem dangerous and exciting. Why not? You only live once. What's the worst that could happen?

These days, people think that if you haven't gone wild, you haven't really lived. College movies depict a constant stream of glamorous parties, hilarious pranks, and fairytale love stories. But we rarely see the real-world consequences of the choices the main characters make. The lifestyle may seem fun, but it often leads to lingering hurt and regret.

You'll never meet people who regret completely devoting their lives to God. How could you regret fulfilling your life's purpose? Your quality of life entirely depends on what you allow to control you and to guide your decisions. "Letting your sinful nature control your mind leads to death. But letting the Spirit control your mind leads to life and peace" (Rom. 8:6).

Who controls your decision making? Do you take responsibility for your actions? Have you ever heard the phrase, "The Devil made me do it"? Wouldn't that be a convenient excuse when you wake up after a night of poor decision making? But can the devil actually make you do something you know you shouldn't?

In *The Screwtape Letters*, C. S. Lewis paints a picture of a more biblical model of temptation and how the devil works. Did you know that Satan isn't God's equal? He's not an ever-present, all-powerful foe. Instead, he ranks as the opposite of the archangel Michael. As a created, finite being, he can't steal our salvation once we've accepted it. The Bible says that once we believe in Christ as our Lord and Savior, God stamps us with His permanent seal of ownership and fills us with the Holy Spirit so we can stand firm and no longer fear the enemy (see 2 Cor. 1:21-22).

But Satan can twist God's truths enough to lure us into a false sense of security until we fall into a trap. As the father of lies (see John 8:44), he's ensnared unsuspecting humans since the beginning. Think about his exchange with Eve in the Garden of Eden. His goal was to convince God's most prized creation to turn against Him. But Satan didn't come right out and say, "Hey, Eve, I think you should disobey God's command and eat from the tree of the knowledge of good and evil. I know God said you'd die if you do, and you'll get kicked out of the garden and be cursed, but hey, doesn't it look delicious?" No, the enemy will never tell us the truth about our precarious position. All he did was ask a simple question that had the ring of reason and let Eve make the decision herself. "Did God *really* say, 'You must not eat'?" (Gen. 3:1, NIV, emphasis added).

Knowing God's word and clinging to His truth helps you ignore Satan when he whispers in your ear about something equally tempting. "Did He really say you have to honor your parents' rules? What do they know anyway? Did He really say to tell the truth about where you were last night? You might get into trouble if you do. Did He really say not to give into your feelings for your boyfriend? As long as you don't go all the way, it doesn't technically count." The Bible describes Satan as a lion on the prowl, actively seeking to destroy all that is holy and good in your life (see 1 Pet. 5:8). Don't let him!

The Holy Spirit gives us the power we need to say no. He will always provide an out. You always have a choice. "God is faithful. He will not allow the temptation to be more than you can stand. When you are tempted, he will show you a way out so that you can endure" (1 Cor. 10:13).

God has the power to crush Satan for good and could do it right now if He wanted to. But He desires to cultivate a real relationship with us, which means we must have the freedom to choose. If we had no option but to follow God, our love would be meaningless. So He allows Satan to tempt us as a test of our faithfulness. Even so, He always acts in our best interest and provides the strength we need to resist the enemy's alluring schemes. He doesn't believe in no-win situations.

But we'll still face strong temptations. Each of us has at least one major weakness that has a death grip on our hearts. Often it's something we fight to keep secret because the shame would destroy us. So Satan hits us from both sides—with sin and guilt. But we can't let it go. Sometimes Satan persists in wearing us down until slipping up seems inevitable.

That's when we need to reach out to God. We can't live righteously by willpower alone. We need help. Things we find impossible are absolutely possible with His help. He works His greatest miracles in areas where we can't succeed on our own. "My grace is sufficient for you, for My power is made perfect in weakness" (2 Cor. 12:9, NIV).

God works to free us from the burden of secret sin by providing an accountability partner, a godly man or woman who knows and loves us enough to tell us the truth, even when it hurts. The enemy uses guilt as a powerful weapon to keep us in chains because we're too ashamed to come clean and confess everything to God. Remember that everyone sins and falls short of Jesus' perfect example and that no one can judge you but the Lord. He already knows what's going on, so why not admit it (at least to Him in prayer) and give Him the opportunity to forgive you and help you to move on? What have you got to lose?

Always be on your guard. Satan can't be in all places at all times, so he chooses his battles carefully. He's most likely to strike when you're the most vulnerable. When you're tired, sick, hungry, or stressed, make sure to stay well connected to God through prayer and devotions. Even if you don't feel like you have the time or energy, it's essential for your spiritual well-being! I know I often make the biggest mistakes or feel the farthest from God when I get distracted and don't spend time with Him for several days.

Also, think about your boundaries in advance. Discuss them with your parents, pastors, or mentors before you leave for college so you have a plan. If you wait to decide how you feel about something until you're in the heat of the moment, you'll be in trouble. Peer pressure, fatigue, emotions, and alcohol can easily coax you into making bad decisions, so be prepared! God not only cares about where you end up but how you got there. So do the right thing, even if it's not easy! Choosing God will always pay off in the end.

The way we live matters. As soon as the people around you realize you're a Christian, they'll watch you to see if your faith makes a difference. If it does, they'll want it too! Similarly, when we yield to temptation, we lose our effectiveness and ruin our credibility. Living in unrepentant sin turns us into one more hypocrite who casts doubt on the reality of God. If He were real, we'd take what He says seriously, and we'd live in a remarkably different way.

Don't get discouraged if your life isn't perfect. No one's is! You've just begun the race, so don't think you're beaten or sure to lose. We all make mistakes, but they're never spiritually fatal if we follow Christ. As long as we're trying our best to live according to His calling and pointing others to Him, God can and will work through us in spite of our failures. Our great and loving God always eagerly offers forgiveness and redemption! "For He has rescued us from the kingdom of darkness and transferred us into the Kingdom of his dear Son, who purchased our freedom and forgave our sins" (Col. 1:13-14).

Remembering three things can help you succeed. First, affirm your relationship with Christ and make sure it's solid. Second, strengthen your relationship with God. To run the race of life well, you need to be well fed, so nourish yourself by reading the Word and going to church regularly. Finally, refuse to isolate yourself from the body of Christ. Going off on your own leaves you more vulnerable to attack. Strong Christian fellowship and accountability will help you stay on track.

Every day you wake up offers a new opportunity to do the right thing. How will you honor and glorify your Lord today?

9
LIVING WITH A MISSION

I always view my life as an adventure in progress. I've grown up reading books and watching movies about unlikely heroes who embark on epic journeys and triumph against all odds. So whenever an unforeseen trial or threat surfaces, it helps me to see it as one more twist in the story God is writing.

My favorite movie trilogy is *The Lord of the Rings*. I went to see *The Fellowship of the Ring* in theaters five times because I couldn't get enough of the thrilling saga. One quote in particular captured my imagination and has served as my personal motto ever since. When Frodo feels overwhelmed with the magnitude of his quest and doubts whether he can succeed, the Lady Galadriel assures him, "Even the smallest person can change the course of the future."[1]

I entered and graduated from college with the mentality that I'd embarked on a mission. I desired to do more than just skate by, take a few classes, and amuse myself. I didn't set out to earn a degree simply because that's what everyone expected of me. I didn't want to do good things with my life. I sought the best the Lord had to offer and pursued it with a vengeance. God has a purpose for my life and strategically placed me at Southern Illinois University Carbondale. Everything I'm doing and enduring is steering me down the path to some glorious finale, and I'll settle for nothing less.

James Emery White perfectly sums up my feelings in his book *Serious Times*. At the beginning, he talks about having a similar passion for epic narratives and declares, "I want to be used profoundly by God, to be seized by His great and mighty hand and thrust onto the stage of history in order to do something significant."[2] We both have a hunger for greatness—not for our own glory but for God's glory. We hope to inspire fellow believers, someday, by being an example of faithful servants through whom God works unbelievable wonders.

Thankfully, we can find inspiration outside the realm of fiction as well. Examples of people who lived life with a purpose fill the pages of history. One of my favorites is William Wilberforce.[3] He didn't start his journey with the goal of glorifying God with his life. Wealthy and worldly, he studied at St. John's College in Cambridge. In 1780, he was elected to Parliament at the age of twenty-one. But he accomplished nothing notable until he gave his life to Christ in 1785. His newfound faith awakened his interest in issues of social justice and morality, and he soon joined the movement to abolish slavery in Great Britain. He faced many setbacks, including a severe, stress-related illness and strong political opposition to each bill he drafted. But he never abandoned his calling, and Parliament signed a bill ending the slave trade on March 25, 1807. William Wilberforce fought for the God-given rights of all men until he died on July 29, 1833. Three days before his death, he learned that Parliament passed the Slavery Abolition Act, which freed all slaves within the British Empire.

Wilberforce took his faith seriously and followed the path God laid before his feet, regardless of the cost. Thanks to his faithful perseverance, God used him to change the world! Believe it or not, you can do the same.

As you progress through your college career, look for ways to act on what you believe. These years will pass in the blink of an eye; time really does fly when you're having fun! Don't get caught up in the minutiae of your day-to-day routine and miss the wealth of opportunities God offers. As James Emery White later says in his book *Serious Times*, "Too quickly, and often without struggle, we trade making history with making money, substitute building a life with building a career and sacrifice living for God with living for the weekend. . . . We become saved, but not seized; delivered but not driven."[4] Never compromise when it comes to your faith. Make every day count.

Living with a Mission

You thrive by standing resolutely on the Rock of your salvation and sending your roots down deep so you're always growing and bearing good fruit. To thrive, means to prosper, flourish, or develop rapidly. But how do you gauge your progress? How do you know if you're headed in the right direction? What's the difference between thriving and just enjoying your time?

Look at the fruit. You can always identify a tree by the type of fruit it bears. Similarly, you'll discover the condition of your heart by seeing what you produce. Picture an orange for a minute. When you squeeze an orange, what comes out? Orange juice. Not grapefruit juice or apple juice. What comes out when you get squeezed? Listen to what flows out of your mouth in those unguarded moments when you are stressed, angry, or surprised. Do you hear loving words from a servant's heart who trusts in the Lord? Or do you find some ugliness that you need to deal with? Good trees can only produce good fruit, while bad trees always produce bad fruit.

Jesus gives us the key to producing good fruit in John 15:

> I am the vine; you are the branches. If you remain in Me and I in you, you will bear much fruit; apart from Me you can do nothing. If you do not remain in Me, you are like a branch that is thrown away and withers; such branches are picked up, thrown into the fire and burned. If you remain in Me and My words remain in you, ask whatever you wish, and it will be done for you. This is to My Father's glory, that you bear much fruit, showing yourselves to be My disciples. (John 15:5-8, NIV)

This book covers several fundamental concepts that will help you cling to the Vine and bear great fruit. I've presented them in the context of starting your college career on the right foot. But they are biblical principles that will allow you continue to thrive through graduation and beyond.

- Cast a greater vision for your life! Figure out what God is calling you to do and see it through to the end.

- Root your identity in Christ and stand firm in His truth.
- Maintain an eternal perspective in all you do.
- Honor God in all your relationships so you may live in harmony.
- Continually seek to know Him better so you'll always be growing and maturing in your faith.
- Be open and vulnerable, allowing Him to transform your life from the inside out.
- Look to Him and Him alone for your security and strength.
- Never settle for less than God's best for your life.

I pray you'll be convicted to live wholeheartedly for Christ so you will be able to walk away from your college experience with no regrets. Life is short. We have no guarantees, so don't put off making this commitment until you're older or ready to settle down and get serious. There is no time to waste, and every minute you choose your own plans and desires over His, you miss out on the best this life has to offer.

He has a purpose in mind for you and wants to get started now. What's He calling you to do today? Where is He calling you to go? Who is He calling you to love?

Go ahead, take a risk. Step outside your comfort zone and allow Christ to lead you on an adventure far beyond anything you've ever asked for or imagined. Cast a greater vision for your future. Start training now so you can run the good race to the end and earn the reward that's waiting for you in heaven. "Therefore . . . let us throw off everything that hinders and the sin that so easily entangles. And let us run with perseverance the race marked out for us, fixing our eyes on Jesus, the pioneer and perfecter of faith" (Heb. 12:1-2 NIV).

Earning a college degree is a marathon, not a sprint, and so is your Christian walk. Take care of yourself so you'll have the endurance you need to finish strong. Keep your eyes on the prize to avoid stumbling and falling. If you do trip, get up and keep running!

Also, invite many others to run alongside you. Think of God's calling as a collegiate Great Commission. "You will receive power when the Holy Spirit comes on you; and you will be my witnesses in

Jerusalem, and in all Judea and Samaria, and to the ends of the earth" (Acts 1:8, NIV). Start to view your campus as your personal Jerusalem. Judea and Samaria represent the New Testament equivalents of your college's city or local community. The ends of the earth means the same thing it did 2,000 years ago: any place on the globe the Lord calls you to go to. Even though you're a college student, God can use you in a big way. "Even the smallest person can change the course of the future," remember?

As you approach the end of your college years, you can help further God's kingdom on your campus in several ways. First, seek out younger students and mentor them to ensure that your community of faith or college ministry will continue to grow and prosper. Think about it like a relay race. Who will you pass the baton to when it's time for you to move on? Pray for the campus and for the churches and ministries in the area, so they may continue the good work that God began there. Also, as you head out into the world and find a new church, get a job, and start a family, consider financially supporting your college ministry with an offering. You can bless future students just as your predecessors blessed you.

Take some time to personally reflect on how far you've come and all that God has taught you and accomplished through you. Has your faith changed the way you live? Are you giving Him your best? Did you ever figure out why God sent you to your university and did you fulfill His purpose? What will your enduring legacy be?

So many problems plague the world, and lost and hurting people need to hear a word from their Creator. He's looking for young people with energy and drive to help Him fix what's broken.

God has given you a mission while you live on earth. What will you do? As for me, I'm going to pray that God will grab hold of your heart, capture your imagination, and take you on the adventure of a lifetime.

> For this reason, since the day we heard about you, we have not stopped praying for you. We continually ask God to fill you with the knowledge of His will through all the wisdom and understanding that the Spirit gives, so that you may live a life worthy of the Lord and please Him in

every way: bearing fruit in every good work, growing in the knowledge of God, being strengthened with all power according to His glorious might so that you may have great endurance and patience, and giving joyful thanks to the Father, who has qualified you to share in the inheritance of His holy people in the kingdom of light.

(Col. 1:9-12, NIV)

RECOMMENDED READING LIST

I would highly recommend all of the books quoted in *A Higher Education*, but I have compiled a condensed list of my favorites for those who are eager for more encouragement in their walk of faith. Happy reading!

- *Celebration of Discipline: The Path to Spiritual Growth* by Richard J. Foster
  This is a classic resource for deepening and enriching your spiritual walk.

- *Crazy Love: Overwhelmed by a Relentless God* by Francis Chan
  It's a quick read that deepens your love and understanding of our amazing Creator and Savior.

- *Destination Unknown: A Guide to Discovering God's Will* by Gordon S. Jackson
  This offers a lot of great, biblically-based advice on seeking God's guidance when you're weighed down with a difficult decision.

- *Good to Great in God's Eyes: Ten Practices Great Christians Have in Common* by Chip Ingram
  As you cultivate a greater vision for your life, this book provides additional inspiration and examples of how great Christians overcome the status quo.

- *A Long Obedience in the Same Direction: Discipleship in an Instant Society* by Eugene H. Peterson
  Learn what it means to truly follow Jesus as you pray through the Psalms of Ascents. These fifteen Psalms were sung when Israel climbed to the top of Mount Zion each year for the great feasts and festivals of the Lord. Their progression mirrors the Christian journey of spiritual growth. Peterson addresses relevant themes for students, like seeking joy, persevering in the face of trouble, and living humbly.

- *Serious Times: Making Your Life Matter in an Urgent Day* by James Emery White
  This is a fascinating look at the cultural challenges Christians have faced throughout history. White looks at the lives of great Christians to help us figure out how to make a difference in this postmodern world.

NOTES

CHAPTER 2

1. Richard Foster, *Celebration of Discipline: The Path to Spiritual Growth* (New York, NY: HarperSanFrancisco, 1978), 1.
2. Frederick Buechner, *Listening to Your Life* (New York, NY: Harper Collins, 1992), 137.
3. Bruce Wilkinson, *The Prayer of Jabez for Teens* (Sisters, OR: Multnomah Publishers, Inc., 2001), 27-28.
4. Chip Ingram, *Good to Great in God's Eyes: 10 Practices Great Christians Have in Common* (Grand Rapids, MI: Baker Books, 2007), 74.
5. Ibid., 75-76.
6. Greg Rohlinger, "Man vs. Wild," (Sermon given at Palm Valley Church, Goodyear, AZ, June 2010).

CHAPTER 3

1. Francis Chan, *Crazy Love: Overwhelmed by a Relentless God* (Colorado Springs, CO: David C. Cook, 2008) 22.
2. "Athanasius of Alexandria," New World Encyclopedia, accessed on 6 March 2010, http://www.newworldencyclopedia.org/entry/Athanasius_of_Alexandria.
3. Eric Ludy, *The Bravehearted Gospel: The Truth Is Worth Fighting For* (Eugene, OR: Harvest House Publishers, 2008), 97.
4. Ben Davenport, quoted in Eric Ludy, *The Bravehearted Gospel: The Truth Is Worth Fighting For* (Eugene, OR: Harvest House Publishers, 2008), 12.

5. Dr. Del Tackett, "Veritology: What is truth?" *The Truth Project*, (Focus on the Family, 2004), DVD.
6. Ibid.
7. Sir William Wallace helped lead the Wars of Scottish Independence and was captured and executed for treason by King Edward I of England on August 23, 1305. He has since become and iconic character of epic poetry and literature, and was famously portrayed wearing blue face paint by Mel Gibson in the 1995 Academy Award-winning film *Braveheart*.
8. Eugene H. Peterson, *A Long Obedience in the Same Direction: Discipleship in an Instant Society* (Downers Grove, IL: IVP Books, 2000) 30.
9. James Emery White, *Serious Times: Making Your Life Matter in an Urgent Day* (Downers Grove, IL: InterVarsity Press, 2004), 98.

CHAPTER 4

1. Richard Foster, *Celebration of Discipline: The Path to Spiritual Growth* (New York, NY: HarperSanFrancisco, 1978), 134.

CHAPTER 5

1. Scott McConnell, "LifeWay Research Finds Reasons 18- to 22-Year-Olds Drop Out of Church," *LifeWay: Biblical Solutions for Life*, August 7, 2007, accessed 5 March 2010, http://www.lifeway.com/Article/LifeWay-Research-finds-reasons-18-to-22-year-olds-drop-out-of-church.
2. Jeffrey Arnold, *The Big Book on Small Groups* (Downers Grove, IL: InterVarsity Press, 2004) 19.

CHAPTER 6

1. Richard Foster, *Celebration of Discipline: The Path to Spiritual Growth* (New York, NY: HarperSanFrancisco, 1978), 1.
2. Ibid., 14.
3. Adele Ahlberg Calhoun, *Spiritual Disciplines Handbook: Practices That Transform Us* (Downers Grove, IL: IVP Books, 2005), 165.
4. Ibid., 165.

Notes

5. Lynne Bujnak and Andy Lang, "Lectio Divina: How to Use the Bible as a Tool for Meditation," United Church of Christ, accessed 19 May, 2011, http://www.ucc.org/worship/calendar/lectio-divina.html.
6. Bruce Wilkinson, *The Prayer of Jabez for Teens* (Sisters, OR: Multnomah Publishers, Inc., 2001), 56.
7. Adele Ahlberg Calhoun, *Spiritual Disciplines Handbook: Practices That Transform Us* (Downers Grove, IL: IVP Books, 2005), 64.
8. Ibid., 64.
9. Richard Foster, *Celebration of Discipline: The Path to Spiritual Growth* (New York, NY: HarperSanFrancisco, 1978), 56.
10. Adele Ahlberg Calhoun, *Spiritual Disciplines Handbook: Practices That Transform Us,* 218.
11. Brandon Steele, "Revelation: Praise God," (sermon given at Ethos Church, Nashville, TN, on April 2011).
12. Eugene H. Peterson, *A Long Obedience in the Same Direction: Discipleship in an Instant Society* (Downers Grove, IL: IVP Books, 2000), 96.
13. Shauna Niequist, *Cold Tangerines: Celebrating the Extraordinary Nature of Everyday Life* (Grand Rapids, MI: Zondervan, 2007), 9-10.

Chapter 7

1. Dr. Del Tackett, "Anthropology: Who is Man?" *The Truth Project*, (Focus on the Family: 2004), DVD.
2. William P. Young, *The Shack* (Newbury Park, CA: Windblown Media, 2007), 142.
3. Frederick Buechner, *Listening to Your Life* (New York, NY: HarperSanFrancisco, 1992), 180.
4. Cathy Sheridan, "It Is Well With My Soul," christianity.ca, Canada's Christian Library Online, (accessed 15 April, 2011).
5. Chip Ingram, *Good to Great in God's Eyes: 10 Practices Great Christians Have in Common* (Grand Rapids, MI: Baker Books, 2007), 122.

Chapter 9

1. "The Mirror of Galadriel," *The Lord of the Rings: The Fellowship of the Ring*, directed by Peter Jackson (Newline Cinema, 2001).
2. James Emery White, *Serious Times: Making Your Life Matter in an Urgent Day* (Downers Grove, IL: InterVarsity Press, 2004), 10.
3. "Why Name the School After William Wilberforce?" The Wilberforce School, accessed 15 April 2011, *wilberforceschool.org*.
4. James Emery White, *Serious Times: Making Your Life Matter in an Urgent Day*, 12.

www.ingramcontent.com/pod-product-compliance
Lightning Source LLC
Chambersburg PA
CBHW060458080526
44584CB00015B/1475